Praise for *This Is Not a Test*

"José Luis Vilson has written a spellbinding book that explains the joys and burdens of teaching. The joys are the kids, with all their heartaches and dreams. The burdens are the politicians and careerists who snuff out the spirits of children and teachers. Read this book!"
—Diane Ravitch, author, *Reign of Error: The Hoax of the Privatization Movement and the Danger to America's Public Schools*

"José Vilson writes from a place of authority about the intersection of race, class and America's education system. His straight talk about the absurdity of America's test obsession, its failure to meet or even acknowledge the needs of an increasingly diverse student population, and a "reform" movement that has reformed nothing, failed at much, and distracted from students' very real needs is a telling portal on what's really going on in American education today. Those who can relate to Vilson's experiences as a student or a teacher will welcome his unvarnished honesty and reflections. And those for whom this is terra incognita will find an insightful and illuminating window on the educational experiences of America's emerging majority—students of many hues and languages, whose families struggle every day, for whom education may be the only way up, yet who too often are failed by systems ill-equipped to foster their success. Vilson's visceral accounts remind us of the humanity of teachers—their struggles and triumphs, their frustration with forces outside their classroom walls and, above all, their devotion to their students. By telling his own story and those of his students, Vilson shows why 'teacher voice' is essential to shedding the failures of the past and to reclaiming the promise of public education."
—Randi Weingarten, president, American Federation of Teachers

"Drawing from his own insight as a teacher, José Vilson hits right between the eyes, exposing how hardscrabble poverty and the pernicious effect of racism distort young lives. In *This Is Not a Test: A New Narrative on Race, Class, and Education*, Vilson argues for more teachers of color, more time for teachers to support each other, and more ways for teachers to shape policy. Bristling at the 'cold calculus' of tests, *This Is Not a Test* calls for practices that engage imagination and respect students as people. In gripping language, Vilson sends students an urgent message: 'When we find our passions, we must enter into them boldly' and believe in the value and gift of ourselves."
—Dennis Van Roekel, president, National Education Association

"In its telling, José Vilson's evocative collection of essays is ferociously honest and, as expected from someone whose creative impulses are

informed by hip-hop, unapologetic and lyrical. A thoroughly engaging narrative about the intersection of race and culture, identity, economic disparity, and education, *This Is Not a Test* is a must-read for parents and educators who want to understand, truly and deeply, the challenges inner-city students face. It was, after all, written by one of those children, a young man from a marginalized community, who grew up and bum-rushed the system he dedicated his life to changing from within."
—Raquel Cepeda, author, *Bird of Paradise: How I Became Latina*

"José's autobiographical journey offers a big window for seeing why our nation must blur the lines of distinction between those who teach in schools and those who lead them. With powerful prose and poetry, his narrative as student and then, later, an NYC teacher leader, loving father (and husband), and advocate for children paints a portrait of what public education can and must be for American society. José's last chapter, 'Why Teach,' offers a hopeful vision for the future of the profession, in spite of wrongheaded policymakers who seek to control teachers rather than listen to and learn from them. José represents so many teachers across the United States whose pedagogical skills and leadership acumen have yet to be tapped in the transformation of teaching and learning. Read *This Is Not a Test* now!"
—Dr. Barnett Berry, CEO and founder, Center for Teaching Quality

"Too many books about teaching read like dull academic treatises, condescending how-tos, or simplistic Hollywood scripts. José Vilson's *This Is Not a Test* avoids these traps with a narrative that is by turns passionate and funny, angry and vulnerable, and full of keen insight born of on-the-ground experience in schools. Whether referencing Jay-Z or John Dewey, discussing corporate school reform or the intimacy of one-on-one interactions with students, Vilson is a bold and fearless writer, weaving his own story and struggles into broader conversations about race, equity, and the future of public schooling. His singular, urgent voice is one we all need to hear."
—Gregory Michie, author, *We Don't Need Another Hero: Struggle, Hope, and Possibility in the Age of High-Stakes Schooling*

"José Vilson is a teacher of the highest order. Through the powerful narrative of his life both inside and outside of the classroom, José teaches us important lessons on every page of *This Is Not a Test*. José teaches us about the intersection of education, race, class and activism while calling all of us to do better—to be better—as we strive along with him to be the educators all our children need us to be. This book is a must-read for educators, soon-to-be educators, parents, students, and anyone who cares about education and the children of this country."
—Chris Lehmann, founding principal, Science Leadership Academy

THIS IS NOT A TEST

A New Narrative on Race, Class, and Education

José Luis Vilson

Haymarket Books
Chicago, Illinois

First published by Haymarket Books in 2014
© 2014 José Luis Vilson

Haymarket Books
P.O. Box 180165
Chicago, IL 60618
773-583-7884
info@haymarketbooks.org
www.haymarketbooks.org

ISBN: 978-160846-370-1

Distributed to the trade in the US through Consortium Book Sales and
Distribution (www.cbsd.com) and internationally through Ingram Publisher
Services International (www.ingramcontent.com).

This book was published with the generous support of Lannan Foundation
and Wallace Action Fund.

Special discounts are available for bulk purchases by organizations and
institutions. Please call 773-583-7884 or email info@haymarketbooks.org for
more information.

Cover design by Eric Ruder.

Printed in the United States.

Library of Congress Cataloging-in-publication data is available.

To the beloved red light and the little defender and warrior.

Table of Contents

"Searching for 'the middle' is pointless—search for truth and let it fall where it will."

—Michael Doyle
@BHS_Doyle

FOREWORD

In today's heated environment, where school reform is at the center of controversy, teachers have cried out for a voice. The decisions that are made far from our classrooms have a tremendous, often deleterious impact on our students, and teachers see the damage up close and personal. As a result, voices from across the country have surfaced to decry the insensitive, painful consequences of the test-and-punish movement. Out of this cacophony rises a beautiful, lyrical voice—one that is uncompromisingly self-aware, reflective, and analytical. That transcendent voice belongs to "The" José Luis Vilson.

I became aware of "JLV" late one night after someone provided a link to his blog. I was taken by the truth, the vulnerability, and the clarity of his writing. It was clear that this man (and there are so few men in the profession, let alone men of color) had a passion for educating children of color. This passion fuels a constant search to make education relevant no matter what. He is a math teacher who can envelop his students in the glow of hip hop while explaining the quadratic formula. As a role model for Black and Latino males, José takes seriously the responsibility placed on his shoulders.

There are a thousand education books you can read, but I think you should read *This Is Not a Test* because of the way José approaches his circuitous journey to becoming a teacher. We get a glimpse of his early life: complicated yet loving, replete with teachers who made an impact on his life. His neighborhood, his walk to school, and his time inside a Catholic-school classroom are so vividly painted that the words jump off the page as his voice keeps ringing, like the school bell calling the children to class.

It is rare that a man this young can demonstrate the wisdom of the ages. He's ready to talk about what it means to be confident when one is supposed to feel shame. He's got stories about his parents—the Dominican mom and the Haitian dad—but his best work comes when he interrogates his own behavior, motives, needs, and desires.

It has been my experience that when conversations about race and class come up, folks run to their respective identity corners. The iniquity of slavery, Jim Crow, and now the New Jim Crow has many folks defensive: "I didn't own slaves." Somewhere in José's narrative he finds a way to say, "But if you benefit from the consequences of slavery, then . . ." He asks hard questions while seeking a way to find solutions, yet he's not afraid to admit when something doesn't work. And while he doesn't shy away from class, this Afro-Latino brother is pure class.

José's dalliance with Teach for America (TFA) and his ability to reflect and synthesize the lessons he has learned from that experience are insightful, as is his keen take on how organizations like TFA, Democrats for Education Reform, and the rest use statistics and numbers to promote vicious policies. José debunks that approach with a quick turn of phrase: "People have grown to equate a number with a fact."

No matter what else you read this year, read this. *This Is Not a Test* is a book that screams against the vagaries of a kind of school reform that ignores the voices of the adults and children who work in public schools. He says, "Our jobs discourage vocalizing dissent, both through individual administrators' intimidation tactics and through formal Internet policies. The hours teachers spend in class and on paperwork also leave little energy for advocacy or political action." But political activity is what it will take to throw off the shackles of oppressive mandates imposed by folks who do not place their own children in test-and-punish institutions.

What José really advocates for is a "fundamental redistribution of power: from a top-down approach to one in which teachers, collectively and individually, take ownership of their roles in reforming education, something our current set of reformers don't all believe is necessary." There it is again, that insistence upon "teacher voice." It's neither whine nor bellow, but a steady trumpeting that resonates with us all. Those of who do the work, have compassion for our students, and know the strengths and limitations of our institutions must have a voice. I await the next book that will explode across the page from José's pen.

Karen Lewis
President, Chicago Teachers Union

On Perspective:

AN INTRODUCTION

> Those children
> should find soft lives
> that drop pendulums in their dreams
> and never tell another story
> about the ghetto
> until they've had to count rats
> with their hands.
> —Tara Betts, "For Those Who Need a True Story"

On the surface, you might assume Tara Betts is telling a story about a kid who, at his mother's behest, kills as many rats as possible so the landlord will lower their rent. Such a tale hits at my very core. I live a little better now, but when my family lived on Clinton Street on the Lower East Side of Manhattan—back when no one wanted to live there—rats came as naturally as breathing and phases of the moon. While the synagogue still called people to worship on Norfolk Street and Katz's Delicatessen became a cultural relic of an older Lower East Side, the 1990s version of the LES had every bit of the street cred that Bedford-Stuyvesant and Harlem did on rap records, without the actual rappers. Roaches scraped crumbs off the floor like poor folks did; killing them symbolized an urban food chain.

When I was maybe four or five, I walked into the bathroom and saw a rat in my tub. I had no experience with killing rats whatsoever, although I'd smelled the faint scent of rat blood, pungent and acidulous, and heard rats pitter-patter behind my walls and under my bed. I tried to wash this gray pup into the drain so it'd scurry like the roaches do, but it stood its ground. This soaked little creature stood there, no bigger than an inch, petrified and shivering, eyes glistening and claws closed to its sides.

I stared at it, then spoke to it for a few minutes. I thought I could befriend it, but the wiser part of me retracted my finger before I could risk catching anything that would make me shiver, too. So we just stayed there, me leaning against the porcelain-coated tub, the rat standing within an inch of an indeterminate sinkhole of escape or death, both of us pondering whether we'd break out of our natural inclination to defend or offend each other's species.

Eventually I called my mom. She ushered me out of the bathroom, told me everything would be okay, and walked back into the bathroom with a sigh.

A few minutes later, she came back out and said the rat was "gone." I'm not sure what actually happened to it, but I know I never saw it again. To this day, I'm still too nervous to ask her.

The parallels between the lives of kids in impoverished neighborhoods and those of rats do not escape me. They help explain why I write as I do. Those who have lived similar experiences to mine understand why we keep a guarded demeanor even when expressing our deepest emotions. We have an unsettling rage beneath our otherwise calm exteriors. Simply walking down the street has been an exercise in survival, even for those of us who consider ourselves nerds or outcasts. The street has taught us not to "snitch"—not because we want to protect the offenders, but because the deaths of people like Amadou Diallo show that even our supposed protectors have something against us. So we speak in folklore, rhyme, and bombast. Tired of waiting for a chance to be heard, many of us have created our own spaces, lest we too get washed down the sinkhole.

I've carried this mentality since doubt became part of my early existence. Before I had the inclination to suck my thumb or walk my first steps, doubt slept under my bed with the monsters and shadows. Many of my family members doubted whether I should have ever been conceived, since I was born of a Haitian man and a Dominican woman. This doubt was followed by the tension of being raised in my early years by a single mother, who pushed me harder than she pushed herself through the plethora of jobs she took to keep herself employed. She eventually filed for disability at a relatively young age. When my stepfather entered the picture, his old-school childrearing mentality led to many irrational beatings and punishments modeled along what we see in Latino Internet memes, like kneeling on rice with my arms out for making too much noise. Outside our home, even if our mothers never ingested cocaine in the seventies and eighties, kids from my generation born into similar circumstances knew that high society widely doubted our survival and didn't care to see how our own government was complicit in our vulnerability. I knew underestimation before I could even spell the word; only confidence, bordering on cockiness, would serve as the antidote.

An amorphous doubt has also showed in people's reactions to me throughout my life, many of whom you'll meet in the following pages. Teachers expected shame but I beamed confidence. Administrators expected fear but I showed bravery. District officials expected quiet but I spoke up. Others expected tears but I refused to shed them.

I remember one incident in the summer of 1996 when, as part of a summer camp program, my eighth-grade diploma newly minted, I had to attend a class on creative writing. I found the class silly, but I didn't want to ruin my momentum by dissenting over something so minor.

The teacher gave us a homework assignment: pick a number and write a poem about it. I struggled for an hour trying to come up with a way to describe the number three, but all I kept hearing was Blind Melon's cover of "Three Is a Magic Number," a *Schoolhouse Rock!* song I could not push out of my cranium for even a second. Perhaps the summer air wouldn't let me concentrate, or perhaps I simply wanted a way out of this assignment, but the next day, when the teacher put his hand out for my assignment, I mumbled, "I didn't do it." Another student had used the number eight's shape as a metaphor for pieces of his life. When the teacher turned back to me, he said, "José, the thing with you is, you're smart and everything, but you're just naturally lazy." My eyes fell out of my head. I wanted to cry—or stuff my face with a grilled-cheese sandwich.

Lazy? How was that even possible? All the plaudits, awards, and well wishes of my teachers only a month before didn't count in this person's eyes. His judgment came down like a hammer when a simple tap would have sufficed. It made me doubt my own writing ability. Looking back, doubt had come in my inability to look at a number abstractly, to consider its shape rather than its value.

As I grew older, my identity as a Black Latino man only made things more complicated. When my mother moved from the Dominican Republic to Miami in the 1970s, she was a young girl trying to please her "tough-love" father. She met my Haitian father working at the same hotel as he did. I would be his only Dominican child, out of the seven children he would eventually have with different mothers. My parents didn't stay together long. My mother moved to the Lower East Side of New York, and my father moved to Flatbush in Brooklyn. My mother thought it gracious to let my father see me, which he did on a yearly basis. But I couldn't capture her grace, her capacity to make people feel welcome, or his charisma, his ability to get people to gravitate toward him.

Miscegenation is in this country's fiber; people fight so hard for the right to love each other regardless of background. Yet I never found solace identifying as Dominican or Haitian. The residue of years of battle between Haiti and the Dominican Republic trickled down to my families, too. As dark-skinned as my Dominican family is, longtime dictator Rafael Trujillo, architect of the Dominican Republic's racial constructs, taught them to see themselves as European as possible. The darkest Dominicans identify with the Taínos, the indigenous people of the Dominican Republic. Anyone who acknowledged their Blackness must have wanted to be Haitian—a serious threat to Dominican nationalism. My Haitian family, having understood this dynamic from the other side of the island, sometimes perceived my distance as snootiness, as if I was looking down at them instead of looking down at my feet.

Living with my mother made me take on more of the Dominican culture, even though a part of me still wishes I could speak *kreyol*.

I swung and spun with the best of the Dominicans on the dance floor, but my facial features didn't resemble other Dominicans they thought they knew, not even the ones who came from predominantly Afro-Latino Santo Domingo. I visited my Haitian grandmother's house in Brooklyn and couldn't understand a bit of kreyol, and had trouble digesting the spices in my grandmother's rice (at least at first). I didn't understand why my brothers, sisters, and cousins on that side couldn't fully accept me, despite looking so much like me.

I have visited the Dominican Republic six times in my lifetime, always thinking I'd find parts of my mother's culture that could make me whole. But I encountered ridicule instead. I learned how to seethe when a child asked eight-year-old me in front of his friends what a *muela* was, and I couldn't remember offhand. When he revealed that it was a molar, the children ran, jumped, and laughed inappropriately hard. The adults fed me pity in tablespoons when I tried to express myself past "*tengo hambre*" (I'm hungry). Imagine if I stepped into Port-au-Prince, Haiti, without a timbre of kreyol in my voice. I never did—and haven't yet. I would have preferred to set up a shack right on the banks of the rivers that split the Dominican Republic and Haiti, countries squabbling politically but at war culturally. I started to set up camp in this hypothetical river when I determined that my skin color shouldn't affect my citizenship to the world around me.

My writing works in the same vein. I've been told that in order for my writing to be universal, it must turn away from things like race or nationality or the conditions of my upbringing. As much as people like the exotic and the erratic on a superficial level, it is even more important to be able to exert order, to be able to categorize those who speak in distinctive voices, to pat them on the head or ignore them completely. I can't allow that. Too many others have felt as I felt, have seen what I saw, have wanted their personhood recognized and their rats counted.

What you're about to read is the most honest account of my life up to this point and how my sense of self has influenced my identity as an educator. As a teacher, I have found that bringing my experiences into my teaching makes the lessons more profound—a connection implicitly highlighted in Paulo Freire's *Pedagogy of the Oppressed*. Freire uses the terms "student-teacher" and "teacher-student," asking us all to think about the cyclical nature of our teaching and learning. Just by living our lives as we do, we become teachers of those experiences. In this book I have chosen honesty over concession, not to launch personal attacks but to provide opportunities for understanding, to fill the holes. As the rapper Immortal Technique once said, "There is usually nothing wrong with compromise in a situation, but compromising yourself in a situation is another story completely." At some point, I saw the little boat I'd been given to row, looked at its bleak destination, and decided I didn't want to end up there.

Father Jack Podsiadlo, my longtime mentor and a father figure to hundreds of students at Nativity Mission School, used to read us the story of Jesus walking on water. In it, the disciples had gone out on a boat at Jesus's behest to come see Him. He appeared to them some time later and walked on the lake to meet them. They were obviously terrified, but Jesus reassured them to take the walk with Him. Peter, the most eager, went out to walk first and started to follow in Jesus's footsteps. However, he let doubt creep into him and soon fell right into the lake.

When Peter yelled out, "Jesus, save me!" Jesus came and helped him back on the boat, but not before asking him why he didn't believe in Him. I took a different meaning from it than perhaps even what Father Jack meant to deliver in his homily: when we find our passions, we must enter into them boldly and trust that we do what we do with a love for that. Right now, and possibly forever, those passions include teaching and writing, and here's my testament to it.

I had to get off the boat so I could walk on water.

Part One

PLEASE PUT YOUR PENCILS DOWN

"What is this test about, Mister?"

"Well, it looks to me like it's the Math Predictive Assessment today."

"So it's a math test? Oh my God, another one!"

"Yes, another one!"

The class I'm proctoring collectively rolls their eyes counter-clockwise.

"What for?"

"Well, this one is to see how much you've learned about math up to this point. The school and your teachers use it to see what you need to learn from here to the actual test."

"Oh."

On January 18, 2012, I had just returned from a nine-day paternity leave, a snowless patch of time I relished with my fiancée, Luz, and our newborn son, Alejandro Luis, who had been delivered at St. Luke's–Roosevelt Hospital on the West Side of Manhattan. (Secretly, Luz had hoped Alejandro and Blue Ivy Carter would share space there; they were born just a couple of days apart.) The little nugget and I had shared tender and intimate moments over those days. The first time I changed his diaper, he peed all over my Fossil watch. The first time he smiled at me, he followed it up with an explosive fart that woke Luz from her nap. The first football game he watched, he put his fist to his forehead and pooped, thus predicting the fate of Tim Tebow's last game of the

2011–12 NFL season against the New England Patriots.

During those days, Luz and I could only tell what day of the week it was by the undershirts Alejandro wore: they literally read *lunes* for Monday, *martes* for Tuesday, and so on. I averaged four hours of sleep, picking up the afternoon and late-night feeding and diaper shifts while Luz took the early morning. Yet I dreaded going back to work. I had my Nugget's face imprinted in the back of my eyelids.

I checked my work email to find out that, upon my return, I would have to proctor an interim math assessment. As a math teacher, I knew I would have to be there, even though I could legally have stayed home another few days. I didn't want to do it.

By "it," I mean the whole spectacle.

A few days before I went back to work, Luz and I discussed Alejandro's options for schooling. When I first moved to Harlem I had come on my own, considering only apartments' aesthetics and proximity to the local and express trains. My child was a speck in my imagination. Now that he was kicking us outside of Luz's belly, we needed to think—and fast.

Quality Head Start programs were likely to cost us a month's combined salary. We saw a few daycare centers that looked welcoming, but the prices scared us. We saw uniformed children of all hues running around our local bodegas and street corners, but there was no way to tell which of them were getting a good education. There's a relationship between how many choices your child has and your income level, and in that we considered ourselves somewhat privileged.

Harlem is one of the flashpoints in the public-school versus charter-school debate raging across the country. It seems that our neighborhood has become an exercise in experimental schooling. Within a few blocks of my house are the Success Academy Middle School, the Harlem Children's Zone, the Harlem Village Academy, the DREAM School with its crisp uniforms and slick advertising, and Democracy Prep—educational institutions that provide a much-celebrated alternative to city schools. Former New York City Council member Eva Moskowitz, who runs the Success Academy Charter Schools network, entices parents by saying that her charter schools are free and public, as if that were somehow exceptional. In fact, charter schools, by their very nature, are *supposed* to be free and open to the public. Geoffrey Canada, founder of the Harlem Children's Zone, also talks a good game about the concept behind his school, including "wraparound services": individualized attention that includes guidance counseling and is partly aimed at kids with special needs. It's a great concept in theory—except that, in real life, entire classes can and will be removed from the school if they do not meet instructional targets. When it comes to the kids and their education, the "school-choice" model is really one of chance.

In the summer of 2013, former New York City schools chancellor Joel Klein told a congregation of centrists and entrepreneurs at the Aspen Ideas Festival that he stakes his legacy largely on the surge of charter schools in the city. This got a rousing applause from all but one audience member. (Guess who?) Calling it a "social justice" issue, Klein repeated the same lines Secretary of Education Arne Duncan and so many others have used: blame the teachers' unions and government bureaucracy for the lack of innovation in public schools.

I don't believe *every* charter school is an attack on the public school system. In fact, some of them are community-developed, a result of central offices telling parents that if they want to build a new school, a charter school is their only option. Yet anyone who believes for a second that Klein, former mayor Michael Bloomberg, or other pro-charter cheerleaders don't have an ulterior motive ought to ask themselves: How can you lead the world's largest public school system, yet rail against it in the same breath? If the problem is really that public schools lack innovation and creativity, why proffer accountability measures that hinder both those things?

As a product of a Jesuit high school education, I have often felt like the "school-choice" movement has marked an awkward transition from religious schools to charter schools. In 2012, Rice High School, the Jesuit Catholic high school and basketball powerhouse in Harlem, closed its doors due to lack of funding. In times of austerity, working with mostly poor Black and Latino kids doesn't turn a profit. What is clear, frankly, is that if you're in Harlem, "school choice" doesn't seem like much of a choice at all. It's either charter or more charter.

It's easy to get the impression that Harlem has embraced charter schools. But the reality is that charter schools have taken over public and private school buildings en masse. The big charter schools advertise themselves to parents as cleaner, better funded, and free. The sense that they are exclusive and thus superior is enhanced by the fact that parents must win a lottery just to get in—parents who see children like their own running around Malcolm X Boulevard in crisp uniforms.

In a perfect world, I could take Alejandro to our local public school a few blocks away, knowing that every teacher would have the same passion and professional qualifications that his parents do.* His school administrators would have the time to learn kids' names while also finding ways to manage constant budget cuts. Every counselor, social worker, and school aide would work with the rest of the school in handling students' social and emotional needs. All of these elements of a great school ecosystem would automatically be in place.

But Harlem seems to have so few of these elements, and in my experience, the average public school doesn't have all of them. Many of my friends from the suburbs—for example, in Scarsdale, New York—tell me that they never had to think about where they would send their children, because the school in the neighborhood was *the* school. The whole community gathers around this school and holds it accountable when it doesn't reflect the community's

---

* Luz is an assistant principal at a transfer high school in Queens and a great teacher, regardless of subject. I might be biased.

values. Teachers are experienced; administrators follow through on the school's vision, which is steeped in tradition. When springtime comes, graduates fall in line to apply to their colleges of choice; even when they can't get into their first choice, they have options commensurate to their needs.

It's hard to imagine a situation in the suburbs where the local NAACP would have to sue the Department of Education to try to end the co-location of charter and public schools in the same building, a practice that creates separate and unequal conditions within a single facility. Yet that's what happened in New York City in 2011. In response to the lawsuit, parents countered that they wanted the same choices that richer families had. But in the suburbs, the local school *is* the school, the lesser choice is still a good choice, and community members can focus their energies on building a school up, instead of tearing each other's schools down.

Also worth noting: Scarsdale parents often remark that they rarely worry about standardized tests.

Speaking of which . . .

"Can I go to the bathroom?"

"Hurry up."

On second thought:

"All the people who have to go to the bathroom: just go now before I gotta sign you out. Hurry up!"

As the procession of boys and girls walks out into the hallway, I look for the special day's roster sheet, sharpened pencils, bathroom log, test booklets, and bubble sheets. I read the test administrator's manual. McGraw-Hill lays out very specific instructions for each grade, each day of testing, and the methods by which its tests must be proctored. We are told exactly what to say and are not to deviate from the script, lest some auditor happen to pass by our school to check our process. I take a breath, partly out of exhaustion from Alejandro's overnight clarion roars, partly out of dread for this grueling process.

"Do you think we're going to pass this test?" Emilia blurts out.

Instead of my mundane answer ("Of course, you'll be fine! And don't worry about it. It's only a diagnostic test anyway!"), I let my inner José out.

"Well, let me see." I flip through the pages. "This one we did, this one we didn't, oh boy, this one, umm, yeah, we did this one, yes, yes, no, no, yes, yes, yes, maybe . . . I'd say about 60 percent of this we've covered."

"Then why do they want us to take it?"

"Because they're mean."

"No, you're mean."

"True, but they're meaner."

They laugh.

"No, seriously, I can't understand why they're making us take this stupid test if they know we're not going to do well on it."

"To be honest, me neither."

"What is this for, anyway?"

Mr. Vilson takes over where José left off. "Well, teachers would like to see what you've learned and what we need to work on in order to get you ready for the big test."

"Oh, I see what you mean. But you think this will help us graduate."

"Well . . ." I waffle here. "Yes, it does." *Fuck.*

"I really don't want to take this test."

"I get it. It'll be over in a few minutes."

Like defendants awaiting sentencing, my kids fidget and scrunch their faces. They know they are about to be locked in a silent, square box for an hour and a half.

"Sir, for how long is this test going to be?"

Angie has taken to calling her male teachers "sir" in a British accent. Unnerving for someone so young, but I'll take it.

"Ninety minutes."

Half the class shifts in their seats. A few kids throw in a "come on," another few go "damn," and one takes the opportunity to fling a piece of paper, or maybe it was the tip of an eraser, at one of his friends. The victim whips around and yells, "Hey, who did that?" I echo the question, much more quietly and with a bit more authority. No one responds. I ask again and look at the usual suspects. Jimmy says, "Yo, why do people always think it's me?"

"Did I *say* it was you?"

"No."

"So why are you so paranoid?"

There's always the one student who does the bad-kid trifecta: shakes the seat, snickers loudly, and yells, "I don't wanna do this bullshit!" Jimmy comes in half an hour late, with one of the deans trailing him. I hear a "get in there" follow him down the chambers.

Mr. Vilson, the professional me, says, "Now, why do we need to yell all that?"

"I don't want to take this test!"

José thinks, *Good, me neither.*

Mr. Vilson says, "I understand, but don't you want to do well?"

"No, I don't want to."

"You do know how important this is, right?" *Not very, kid.*

"I don't care!"

"Yes, you do." *We don't either.*

"I wanna go home!"

"Now, is it necessary to make all that noise while we're trying to start this test?" *Rebel! Please rebel!*

"Fine, I'm going to put my head down because I'm not doing this shit!"

"Okay. I'll still have your test ready for you." *It hurts us almost as much as it hurts you.*

I start maneuvering through the aisles, around desks perfectly aligned in units, handing out bubble sheets and exams with natural ease. I start reading the instructions: "Today, you will take the New York State Interim Examination in Mathematics . . ." One kid moves a bit, then stops after I pause and look in his general direction. "You will have ninety minutes to complete this examination. Use only a number-two pencil; do not use a pen. Make heavy black marks. Do not make any stray marks and erase any such marks completely. Please make sure you use all the time allotted and answer all questions completely. When the time is up, please put down your pencils as it is the end of the exam. If you look at the bottom of the page and see the words 'Go on,' please go on to the next page. When you see the word 'Stop,' that is the end of the exam. During the time allotted, you may go back and check your work."

"Are there any questions?" I suspire and then wait five seconds.

In those five seconds, I wonder if we can do this testing ritual better. Gouging my eyes out doesn't feel like the most productive use of the next eighty-nine minutes. At the same exact time, across the whole city, thousands of teachers must be contemplating the same thing. For an average of three hours a day during the six-day ritual of examination from the city, plus the six to ten days of official exams from the state, teachers miss out on actually teaching the students. Technically, the actual testing time is roughly 5 to 7 percent of the school year; in reality, though, it takes much more than that. Teachers have to keep said tests in mind when they prepare their lessons, just in case a certain question shows up, and the whole school system is centered around whether we can bump the numbers up from one standardized test score to the next, down to the hundredth percentage point. With all the discussion about "closing the achievement gap," curricula, and standards, policy makers rarely take input from the people who need classroom time the most: teachers.

"You may begin."

Actually, policy makers rarely ask us anything until after they've pushed their tools upon us: thumb drives full of PowerPoint presentations replete with graphics and logos, mile-high piles of manila folders emblazoned with yet more logos, teams of twenty- and thirty-somethings brimming with ambition (but with an average of only three years in the classroom), sets of acronyms for us to memorize and decipher on our own. Our input might get them to change the wording on one or two sentences in their packets, but when it comes to implementing policy, the rest of the game plan remains the same. Anyone with even a modicum of experience with central offices knows this.

In a sense, it almost feels like a pyramid scheme: the structure rarely loses form, even as bricks within it shift. We're not working with bricks, though. We're working with people, many of whom have great ideas, and the current educational paradigm rests on our collective shoulders.

So why do we concede to be subservient test proctors? Do we offer our own alternatives or develop our knowledge of pedagogy and practice to challenge inexperienced wannabes who claim to know better? Do we exercise our First Amendment rights only in the confines of our anonymous blogs and teachers' lounges or do we proactively enumerate—and address—our grievances through coalition-building? Do we see the relationship between the working conditions of teachers and the learning conditions for children? Can we counteract claims that teachers ought to separate the emotional and the professional by integrating our passions into the work we do? As a society, can we rationalize the seemingly endless deluge of uninspired assessments for our kids?

Can we create a balance between developing better students and inspiring better people? *Please?*

"You have ten minutes to complete this test."

Annoyed at spending an hour and a half on an interim test that won't tell us very much, I look in the test booklet and mentally do the questions myself. I get 95 percent correct without scrap paper in just under seven minutes. I survey the students: most of them completed the test about twenty minutes ago. Some heads rest on their graphite-scuffed desks, snores blowing against pencils that drop to the floor. The creatives use the backs of their tests as canvases while the drummer from the school band taps his pencil against the desk to the tune of LMFAO's "Party Rock Anthem" before I give him the teacher look for the umpteenth time. I whisper that it's appropriate for them to recheck their answers now, trying to keep their minds occupied for the next minute.

I can't help but feel that when my students walk out of their exams, they aren't just frustrated by the inordinate amount of testing they're subjected to. They're starting to sense that the process of schooling in and of itself was not actually designed with them in mind—a feeling those of us born into poverty and racism know all too well.

By teaching students of color that the best way to succeed is to respond to tests the way the state demands, determine the validity of an argument under the state's rules, and examine essays only if they follow the state's standards, we are creating education via deculturation, or stripping a culture, instead of transculturation, the merging of cultures.

We didn't land on education reform. Education reform landed on us.

But these thoughts are for another time. "Please put your pencils down," Mr. Vilson says. "You have completed your test."

José thinks, *Actually, far from it.*

CAN IT BE THAT IT WAS
ALL SO SIMPLE THEN?

"And what's *your* name?"

My first real school was PS 140, on the corner of Ridge and Rivington Streets, on the Lower East Side of Manhattan. I went there from 1986 to 1994, pre-K to sixth grade.

It was a tall, gray marble-and-brick building with an intimidating playground, auburn doors, and kids three times my size. The school had a smaller and better-decorated playground, set apart specifically for little cubs like me to insulate us from the "big-kids'" playground, a seemingly vast space with jungle gyms, handball courts, a basketball court, and a huge middle space for just about anything from makeshift Wiffle Ball to a fifty-person game of tag.

Almost every wall of the school was bordered by either a school park or a garden. The dark alleyways in between were full of vines and dumped crack vials—a common pathway for people who dealt in nickel and dime bags. Grass and plants tangled with tall, black, pyramid-tipped iron spikes, decorating the front of the school, an entryway with a few stairs and six gray doors. Around three every afternoon, kids rushed out the doors and the streets were flooded with preteens in Jordans and Keds, channeled by adults in ties or police-like blue uniforms.

The brown rotunda across the street (PS 142) didn't seem that different from my school. I didn't understand the words

21

"zone," "choice," or "rate of student achievement" or what they had to do with two schools separated by a street and a digit. We knew of Our Lady of Sorrows, an elementary Catholic school just a block away from PS 140, but we already had *our* school. If we wanted to go to OLS for religious reasons, we attended the Saturday program for confirmation and communion. My mother trusted the principal at PS 140 more, so that's where we landed. I couldn't have foreseen that the predominantly Jewish and Puerto Rican veteran school teachers at PS 140, who had seen the tumultuous and triumphant moments of the New York City public school system, would do so much to prepare us early on for our future academic challenges.

On my first day of school, I woke up to my usual routine: a big bowl of Frosted Flakes, some juice, and cartoons on TV.* With my glasses pushed to the bridge of my nose and my mom walking me to school, I felt a little comfort knowing that our small apartment was a block away: if I had to, I could run back to my oasis and patiently wait for my mom on the stairs. I walked through the school doors and found my way into a green-tiled room with two sinks and a ton of kids waiting for instructions from an older lady named Ms. Sussman.

"What's *your* name?"

"José."

Ms. Sussman asked us to form a large circle for an icebreaker. We sat cross-legged ("Indian style," as we called it then) and listened as our classmates introduced themselves. At some point during the eighth or ninth person's turn, I caught a wave of "yuck." It seemed like the people in front of me started swaying back and forth. I couldn't call out because that might be rude to the person speaking, and I didn't want to be *that* jerk. But then I found a salmon-colored substance flowing out of my mouth and nose.

---

* Along with daily Our Fathers and *pidiendo bendición* (seeking a blessing) from my mother.

I barfed, covering half of the makeshift circle by the time I finished.

Kids stared at me with piercing, wary, judgy eyes. That was my introduction to schooling. Before I could even spell the word, I had already taken an antisocial stance against the establishment. My eight-year commitment to that big gray building suddenly felt like forever. *And ever.* And I had better get used to it or society might never let me into any doors.

For the next eight years, my classmates and I rushed through six gray entrance doors, up the small staircase that led up to the lobby, past the observant, chatty security guards, and right into the lobby. We waited in the cafeteria for our teachers to pick us up and bring us to class, gnawing on breakfast bits from the free breakfast program, staring at the glass-protected display of the month, glancing at the attendance records to see whose was the highest. We discussed Michael Jordan's ridiculous play against the New York Knicks. Then we lined up and walked through the pristine burgundy hallways and into our respective rooms. We would read in the morning and write a short reflection about what we read; then, when the bell rang, we'd switch to math with the same teacher. She'd teach us most of the topics of the day, unless it was science with Ms. Miller or computer class with Ms. Schlesinger.* We got a decent amount of homework, then left for the day. (By decent, I mean I still lean a little more forward from the boulder-weight books I carried in my bookbag.)

Can it be that it was all so simple then?

◆

In those years, students across the nation presumably got the same education I did. They either sat in single-row, single-file or in clusters

---

* Ms. Schlesinger's class inspired me to become a computer scientist. She always had the coolest stuff in the school: the new Apple computers, the first dial-up connections, the interactive games. On the other hand, she once told me after I experimented with her computers, "You don't know everything!" Pfft. Watch me.

for group projects. They had colorful posters all over the walls, with cursive-letter strips above the blackboards for lower- and uppercase letters. They had the pushover teachers, the warm but demanding (and sometimes downright scary) teachers. They had parent/teacher conferences where students might be described as "struggling," a list of deficiencies rattled off. Our teachers covered everything from gossip to hygiene.

My school back then always felt solid. We had a strong principal and a great staff. The lunches generally tasted fresh, outside of a few undercooked string beans. We got regular visits from a semi-famous person or company, ostensibly to motivate us but also to show just how important we were. Our principal always lauded our school for our math, reading, and attendance ranking in the district.

I didn't know that the delicate relationships between principal, administrators, and fellow teachers can make or break a school environment, or that added stressors like budgets, test performance, and surrounding neighborhood activities only intensify those relationships in the building. Average spending per pupil for New York State in the early 1990s—when I attended PS 140—was around $7,600, but New York City only saw a $4,498 average.

As an adult, I once looked in the paper and found PS 140 on the list of persistently dangerous schools in New York State as of 2007. Even after it was removed from the list in 2009, I couldn't believe it. In the eighties and nineties I had always felt it was safe and believed I was getting the best education possible. My naïveté was a byproduct of the limited scope I had as a child. But things also change in two decades—including an entire profession.

In many ways, such a school feels atypical today. Had our current heightened accountability measures been in place then, they would have likely snipped the warm-and-fuzzies I felt walking down those hallways. The school building may feel the same and the classrooms may not have changed much, but can a school preserve a warm environment when it is beholden to the cold calculus of keeping up test scores?

Individually, the way teachers remember their years in school is often indicative of how they view "good" education, even if it didn't really work for everyone. It always starts off the same: "When I was a student, teachers used to _____, and we'd learn because _____, and that's why I do it that way." Some school leaders believe that asking their teachers to think back to the way they were taught could reveal the key to *every* student's education. We could fill those blanks in with the most inane practices and people within earshot would nod and say "YEAH!" and "Something similar worked for me, too!" Here's a snippet of some actual dialogue I've heard in a teachers' lounge:

> Teacher A: "When I was a student, my teacher used to draw lettuce next to the most important points of her notes and that worked because I could identify with lettuce and it would get us all hungry so we'd want to work harder for that lettuce!"
>
> *What did she just say?*
>
> Teacher B: "I'm with you! I had one teacher who put on a clown face whenever we discussed books like *Of Mice and Men* and *Flowers for Algernon*. I really understood the book then, and the rest of the class enjoyed it too!"
>
> *José, if you just smirk, it'll all go away.*
>
> Teacher C: "Well, my original language is French, and based on what my teacher said, he speaks the best French and there really is no other French that makes sense to me. And when I learned it, I knew it was the best because people would tell me how great it is, so there I go."
>
> *Oh hell no.*

Rather than mumbling under my breath, I should have asked, "Are you sure every kid in your classes actually learned?" Most of us in the teaching profession have a great collective mentality, but one of the major failures of "groupthink" is assuming every teacher who agrees with us is a reincarnation of the average student we grew up with. It's just not true. Logically speaking, people who participate in this type of this discussion are saying that almost everyone who is within our age range, income level, education level, and profession learned the material exactly that way and that's why it was so effective.

Every generation of students has its set of social signifiers and, within individual classrooms, a language apart from the standard that exists throughout the rest of the school. As a teacher, for example, to get students' collective attention, I used to count down, "Five . . . four . . . three . . . all eyes on me." The second I said it, someone inevitably echoed, "ALL eyes ON me," with an imitation 2Pac voice. I would make a teacher face at the student who echoed me, but was encouraged by the wit nonetheless. Another example: When I ask students to turn to a page in our textbooks, start from the bottom, and work their way up, someone always cuts me off and says, "Started from the bottom, now we here!" Drake didn't start from the bottom, but he ended up in my classroom because I said those words.

Would I have struck that nerve in a school without a bit of hip-hop knowledge? Perhaps not. Do I still teach math "properly"? It depends on context and audience, largely. Classrooms require teachers to get to know their students before trying to teach them anything else, and this is no less true where the students are hardest to teach. In no way do I suggest buying a Lil Wayne record and incorporating his slang into the classroom, but our students have a culture that's both authentic and unique to them. If you can tap into that energy, you have a way to reach them in ways that even our own teachers couldn't.

As educators, what we could say is, "My teacher taught me this way and it worked for me and a few of my friends, so that's why I'm teaching this way." We could also take it a step further and say, "I'm open to other, possibly more effective ways of teaching the material based on real research and improving my pedagogy to reach the most children possible." We can own up to the idea that that the people attending those meetings usually were the "good" kids in their elementary-school classes.

I have thought about every kid I shared a class with in elementary school, middle school, and high school. I don't know that I considered whether they had learned the material as well or better than I did. Did I think the whole class was doing as well as I was? Remembering the faces my teachers made after they handed back our quizzes, probably not.

Self-motivation is important, of course. Throughout my elementary years, I read voraciously and sought to show off my skills via quizzes and tests. Since I had no access to my father's native kreyol, I wanted to make absolutely sure I knew more than enough Spanish to stay in conversation with my mother's family. So I taught myself how to read and write in Spanish using the New Testament. The ways I learned out of school translated to how I learned in school, which often made the process of schooling boring. Did I side-eye the winners of the "best homework" awards at the year-end school ceremonies? Absolutely. Was I jealous? Yes, to an extent. Maybe I just thought that my work ethic didn't match my intellect because I . . . well, I learned better when I went at my own pace, which was anything from a jog to warp speed depending on whom you ask.

But students' paths also get determined from a young age in a way that doesn't always encourage self-motivation. New York elementary schools split students up into three to four classes, often separating the lowest and highest achievers. With a few switches here and there, students get tracked as a unit until middle school, where the shuffle happens again, this time with a different principal and a different set of students who may or may not recognize each other from the neighborhood. (These days, "school choice" has made it so that a school may get students right from the neighborhood or a few miles away, depending on the central district's calculations.)

After eighth grade, students put twelve high schools on a list and hope to get caught in the web of one of them. Otherwise, they fall down the cracks to a second round of lotteries. During this fuzzy period, students start to see the writing on the wall. Those with strong grades usually get chosen for their first-choice high school; students with weaker grades have to attend the "default" school, usually a school pegged for low expectations and more open admissions. The high schools' names often feature a specialization like medicine, art, or law, but most offer the same exact courses with very few variations, according to some of my former students.

The architecture doesn't exactly motivate students to come to school. Most of the large high schools that have been broken up into smaller schools share facilities like the gym, the cafeteria, or the classroom, a transparent flaw of the smaller-schools movement. The entrances still have police guards and metal detectors, and windows still have tight-grid window guards. The hallways are still dimly lit and painted in the most uninspired colors possible.

Today, browsing my yearbooks and Facebook friends, I have a good sense of who among my elementary-school classmates went to college and who didn't. Some started families early on, moved to another state, entered the military or law enforcement, or got other service jobs just to maintain a good standard of living. Others stepped (tripped?) into lots of trouble, sold or used drugs, and still battle their inner *demonios* to get to the next day. The characteristics that lead to success are such volatile variables. A few of us may be successful by society's definitions (rich or famous), but seeing what I did growing up, my definition of success has to accommodate people who are generally managing to live fruitful, positive lives.

Who gets to write their edu-memoirs? How would my classmates speak to their educational experience? Would they feel the same way I do? Why do we place so much emphasis on *just* effort if we know that any number of factors can affect a student's personal journey through school? As children we are told repeatedly that we need only the wherewithal to survive and excel in the business of schooling. As adults who were once those children, we ought to see that the combination of events, no matter their size, that got us to our present is what put us on our life's eventual trajectory.

BAND OF BROTHERS

When someone asks me if I ever joined a frat, I tell them the same story: "I considered a few when I was in college, but that time's passed. I'm good." Fraternities may serve a purpose for some and I certainly had an interest in a few, especially of a purple-and-gold variety. I shrug casually, because the person who usually asked me either joined such an organization or has considered doing so. Then I think about the other colors and values I'm associated with, and am relieved that I already have a whole network of people bounded by this set of experiences through a small Catholic middle school on the Lower East Side.

One night in 2011, I got to hang out with this band of brothers for my good friend Victor Cirilo's "Washington, DC or Bust" party at Slainte's, an Irish establishment on Bowery Street in the East Village. As I looked around, with Biggie's "Juicy" blaring through the bar speakers, I reminisced about my years at Nativity Mission School, an independent Catholic middle school on the Lower East Side. Located on Forsyth Street and aimed at serving underprivileged youth from the neighborhood, the former apartment building might not look so remarkable from the outside. But anyone who has spent even ten minutes inside during a regular school day can't miss it.

I thought about the red brick, the black fire escapes, the concrete backyard with the odd hoops, the seemingly endless staircases, the metal park table, the storage closet, the Ping-Pong table, the basement you never wanted to go into unless that Ping-Pong ball dropped down the stairs. The washing machines for the boys' sports uniforms, the tight spaces that assured no one could ever get lost, the little closet that held basketballs and our student shop, and the walls that housed classes for the last three decades.

◆

During the summer months every year from 1994 to 1998, I attended a six-week program that was associated with Nativity Mission at Camp Monserrate on a private property in Lake Placid, New York. Designed to provide leadership training for current and prospective Nativity students, the program involved hiking up the largest peaks in New York's Adirondacks mountain range, along with canoeing, swimming, and prayer. It was a huge departure from summers in the city—and it was during those summers, in one of our evening sessions, that I was first introduced to the movie *Stand and Deliver*. Starring Edward James Olmos as Jaime Escalante, the acclaimed mathematics teacher in East Los Angeles who got his high-school students to learn *cálculo* against all odds, the film was unlike anything I had ever seen. Father Jack showed it to us every summer, trying to inspire us to achieve the seemingly unachievable. It was just one of the ways in which our trips to that grassy ridge in Lake Placid gave Latino boys from the city a chance to see something they might not have otherwise. We ate grilled-cheese sandwiches and pork chops with a refreshing cup of lemonade—keeping our elbows off the table or else we wouldn't get seconds. We swept floors with our bare hands, learned how to make our beds with folded ("hospital") corners, and took five-minute showers. Camp was our pledging and if we roughed it out, we made it. Young men like us had no choice but to give it our all.

Along with introducing me to Jaime Escalante, it was Father Jack who prompted me to use my gifts to improve myself, not to harbor hate for others. During the school year, he drove me to my spelling bees, making sure to slip in a few lessons about life on the way. Maybe it was because he heard so many of our confessions or because he spoke what seemed like thirty languages, but he had a way about him that could pull the most anxious among us off the ledge.

♦

"If you look at your teaching career, you've been trying to create that Nativity experience ever since you started," Luz said to me one day.

She has a way with words, too.

For all my years of schooling, more than any other institution, Nativity taught me about *myself*. I learned about the fourteen Stations of the Cross from my Saturday Catholic school at Our Lady of Sorrows, but I found my spirituality from Nativity. Xavier High School completed my learning of Jesus's teachings, but Nativity pushed me to the idea of walking on water.

Even now, while the redbrick building has slowly been deconstructed and in its place lies the frame for a high-rise condominium in a neighborhood twelve years deep into gentrification, the spirit of Nativity still remains where two or more of us are gathered. The Lower East Side still retains the small clothing shops on Orchard Street, Katz's Delicatessen, the projects near the East River (maybe), and the Nuyorican Café. But Nativity could no longer state its purpose to be helping the poor after the poor were forced to flee to less prosperous and inflated properties. Nativity as an institution had to move somewhere it could retain its mission statement; Nativity as a building felt more isolated.

The cohesion of these boys turned men, some of whom may not know or like each other, is centered on the image of the little school that could. Father Jack keeps saying that Nativity isn't a building but a community, made up of the generations of people affected by this meek institution, no matter how much we protest. Nativity was, and is, about paying service forward, and its leaders hope to find a place where they can build a new legend and a new bond with kids who otherwise wouldn't have a chance.

Years later, I would find myself trying to do the same for my students.

WHAT HAPPENED

Harlem winters still showcase full moons above 116th Street and Malcolm X Boulevard at 6:30 a.m., just to the side of the dome of Clara Muhammad Elementary and Secondary School. As I walk the silent, tenebrous streets toward the C train, my iPod plays Kanye West's "Dark Fantasy." The thump of the bassline in step with my pace sets the mood. With the second verse, he piques my curiosity with an interpolation of Slick Rick's "Teacher, Teacher."

> Hey, teacher, teacher
> Tell me how do you respond to students?
> And refresh the page and restart the memory?
> Respark the soul and rebuild the energy?
> We stopped the ignorance, we killed the enemies . . .

My vigorous head-nodding pauses just long enough for me to reflect on these lines. Did he just provide a framework for the future of pedagogy for our students, particularly those most disenfranchised by this system?

In reflecting on my own education, I often reiterate the many ways my own teachers helped me mature as a student, but I also had experiences that occasionally make me wish I had openly rebelled. Most students take a passive-aggressive route to defy their teachers, which really works to teachers' advantage because it doesn't require them to reconsider what in their pedagogy might have incited such a reaction. Despite the plethora of studies and papers written about teachers as learners (Paulo Freire comes to mind here*), the top-down structure of schooling has long stifled independent thought.

I first became aware of this in seventh grade, when a discussion with my language-arts teacher, Mr. Missile, became an argument. A tall man with a sharp voice known for his coffee thermos resembling a weapon of mass destruction, Mr. Missile always had a nervous twitch probably from too much caffeine. None of us dared question it. One day, he gave our class a well-deserved three-minute break at the end of the period. As seventh-grade children are wont to do, we chatted among ourselves about the NBA, video games, or anything else that took our minds off the rigors of schooling, getting louder and louder with each passing minute. Mr. Missile called out to me with something I couldn't hear, and I responded with, "What happened?"

That was apparently a big mistake. Mr. Missile corrected me, and said, "You ought to use 'Excuse me' instead." I couldn't hear that either, so I said, "What happened?"

"José, again, you need to use 'Excuse me.'"

"Wait, what happened?"

"José, if you don't stop it, for every time that you use 'What happened,' I'm going to make you write it a hundred times."

At this point, my classmate Aquiles just kept shaking his head at me and saying, "Oh my God, no!" I didn't hear any of what Mr. Missile said to me, but they were under the impression that I did.

"What happened?"

"One hundred . . ."

"What happened?"

"Two hundred . . ."

---

* Freire, a Brazilian scholar and author of the best-selling *Pedagogy of the Oppressed*, attempts to reframe education as a progressive transfer of power. Instead of a top-down teacher/student dynamic, Freire proposes that everyone in the system, from students to the community, has something to learn from one another, thus creating increasingly more fluid titles for entities in the classroom based on needs of the surrounding community.

"What happened?"

"Three hundred . . ."

By the time he'd counted to 1,100, Aquiles was practically jumping out of his desk to stop me.

I was in shock. "What happened?" felt appropriate because I actually wanted to know what had happened. Apparently Mr. Missile preferred "Excuse me," a term I would have reserved for passing by someone. Later that night, after finishing all my real homework, I started my punishment assignment at 9:30 p.m. My mother peeked in to see what I was up to, but I had a hard time explaining in my broken Spanish what had happened. After line 839, I didn't see the point of the assignment, only that I had been punished for waxy ear canals and temporary idiocy. By line 1,099, my hands pounded the table where, through my clenched teeth, I said, "Make. It. Stop."

By line 1,100, the assignment had worked: Mr. Missile had, even temporarily, stifled the phrase, shoving it into the deepest recesses of my vernacular. More importantly, I had unconsciously run into the dichotomy between schooling and education.

Education should be the set of actions and processes by which educators, students, and parents work together to help future citizens succeed and contribute to general society. Egalitarian as that sounds, most people I've spoken to believe in that vision in one form or another. On the other hand, we have this concept of schooling as a set of procedures that happen in a continuum, irrespective of (and often despite) whether the students actually learn anything, like commuter trains running on a schedule. I could blame Mr. Missile's punishment on a misunderstanding, but I also see it as symptomatic of the schooling process, which often fails to account for other children's literacy, as if the code that children speak has no value compared to the King's English. The train must keep going, even if the passengers don't want to hop on.

The cultural and class disconnect between many educators and their students is as much to blame for the countercultural movements among some kids of color as any other influences. Social conservatives often point to current rap music's misogyny and violence* as the reason why today's kids don't pay attention to their teachers, or any adult for that matter, yet there is a long tradition of rap and hip-hop inspiring young people to seek an education—not a schooling, mind you—that schools could not always provide. That goes for public, private, or any type of school.

In the mid- to late nineties, rap albums displayed an ostensible anti-intellectualism that encouraged bucking formal schooling as a measure of success. In 1991, a nineteen-year-old Busta Rhymes admitted to early mischief in "The International Zone Coaster" with "No need to make bets 'cause I met a bookie/Today is the day the whole school plays hooky." Later in the 1990s, the Notorious B.I.G. did this in "Juicy" when he quipped that "this album is dedicated to all the teachers who told me I'd never amount to nothin'." As recently as 2011, Jay-Z did the same in "Who Gon' Stop Me":

> Graduated to the MoMA
> and I did all of this without a diploma
> graduated from the corner
> y'all can play me for a muthafuckin' fool if you wanna
> Street-smart and I'm book smart
> coulda been a chemist cause I cook smart

These Brooklyn kids all went to the same high school around the same time, became extremely successful by their early twenties, and found themselves revered in pop culture not for their obvious intelligence but for their musical talent.

In other words, while schooling might have worked for some, it obviously failed some intelligent yet distracted children of color who had to find other ways to express their discontent with the schooling they received. The lure of their message is how it dismisses

---

* Not to excuse rap's issues with these -isms, but white-dominated forms of music also have binders full of issues with misogyny and violence. Worse still, even if we don't "see" it in the music, it's often permissible in backstage VIP areas at concerts and clubs, off-campus houses, or concert mosh pits under the guise of drugs and rock culture. Alas.

the schooling narrative of "If you work hard, behave good, and get good grades, you'll do well in life." That's true for many, but our most disaffected students don't see themselves in the curriculum and thus have to find their own outside of school. Kids today have the correct impression that people have more fun outside of school, yet few adults ever think about actually changing the schooling so kids can get an education.

Children of color have had a different, unjust education, even before this current education reform—public, private, or otherwise—and this is how many of our children choose to respond.

Other People's Children, by world-renowned education scholar Lisa Delpit, articulates this problem well and offers solutions. Reading the chapter titled "Language Diversity and Learning," I couldn't get past how much of it reflected my own experience. She writes, "Teachers need to support the language that students bring to school, provide them input from an additional code, and give them the opportunity to use the new code in a nonthreatening, real communicative context."* When students bring a different understanding of the English language into the classroom, teachers need to be able to look past the difference in usage so that they can see students' competencies and ideas. Without realizing it, Mr. Missile's approach to language arts only fueled my abandonment of the English canon. Harder to swallow was his role in questioning my code of English, positioning himself as owner of the true, authentic version.

I did well academically, but I was still antisocial and a misfit; even my teachers probably found this brown know-it-all-who-probably-just-needed-some-guidance a bit obnoxious. I knew of hip-hop the way we know of expensive clothes behind pristine glass windows. When I sneaked in listening sessions of hip-hop radio station Hot 97 in my bedroom, I felt it in my bones—not because I ever dealt drugs or shot a man with a .38 pistol, but because I lived in a neighborhood where I saw and heard it all myself far too often. I felt the underlying anger of these young men who, behind their bravado and hypermas-

---

* Lisa Delpit, *Other People's Children* (New York: New Press, 2006), 53.

culinity, revealed a sore spot in their hearts because they felt the world around them didn't actually belong to them.

For a month or two, I found myself disenchanted with schooling. In some respects I stopped participating altogether. I eventually developed a "me against the world" mentality—appropriate for the spring of 1995, when 2Pac released an album with the same name. When I listened to it, something about his critique and social rebellion felt real to me.

Comparisons between hip-hop and the classroom abound. Hip-hop has different forms of "response" that the traditional classroom doesn't allow. In response to a song, people can dance, mimic, remix, or cover it with their own lyrics. They can draw or write. Rap music asks us to pay careful attention the first time, but express ourselves by the second time we hear it. Language flourishes in real time. The next time we convene to listen to the song with our friends or at a party or concert, we need not assess whether everyone knows it all. Rap turns the whole idea of standards on its head by saying, "You need skill to do what I do, but if you enjoy what I do, you do what you do. As long as you got soul, you're in."

In other words, I belonged here. Some educators in America still leave admittance to the process of schooling up for debate.

Some children might thrive in traditional schooling because their particular talents and ethics are a good match for that environment. But many others simply don't. They become denizens of the corner, the hustlers of rap lyrics. Schooling builds a dichotomy between those for whom schooling works and those for whom it doesn't. Those of us who play in both worlds become linguists just by discerning between the English spoken in the schools and the English spoken by the broke, because I refuse to call it "broken English." Because I prefer code-switching.

Yet I write. In many versions of English. In the face of resistance from the official arbiters of language, many of us can still read and write English well.

You might even wonder what the hell happened.

NEGOTIATING MY OWN SKIN

As children, we didn't understand what "difference" meant system-ically.

We saw teachers come bright and early to prepare their class-rooms, placing desks in circles or in rows. We saw clean hallways, more often than not, and administrators waiting out in front of the school, waving at parents and community members. Taking tests, while no thrill, didn't stress us out too much because our teachers assured us they just wanted to compare what we had learned with others.

School was school—until we got to see what life was like past the Hudson River.

In the 1990s, most of my friends tuned into *The Fresh Prince of Bel-Air*, the sitcom starring Will Smith as a poor kid from a rough neighborhood adjusting to life in the affluent Los Angeles neigh-borhood of Bel-Air with his uncle Phil Banks and aunt Vivian Banks, both successful professionals. While *The Cosby Show* had spoken to the African American experience and tried to cast mid-dle-class Black life in a positive light, "Fresh Prince" spoke to a culture clash and escapism that resonated with us in the same way Eric B. & Rakim's "Paid In Full" had for the previous generation. We had never seen affluence firsthand, but mansions and preppies made their way into our vocabulary through these shows.

Along the way, television also showed us what school looked like for rich folk. When Will Smith's character strolled through

Bel-Air Academy, we saw wooden walls and shiny tiled floors and assumed it had open spaces that allowed for sports other than basketball and street baseball. Carlton Banks, Uncle Phil's not-Black-enough son, worked as Will's foil, the product of the American dream yet stripped of the grounded sense of Black history. While he succeeds easily at the process of schooling, his real education comes from his shocking encounters with Will's disruptive personality.

Thus, through the relationships between Will and Carlton—and Will and Phil—*Fresh Prince* speaks directly to the struggles chronicled in the writings of Carter G. Woodson, specifically *The Mis-Education of the Negro* (1933). In the book, Woodson describes the education system as a means of programming people's worldviews. If Bel-Air Academy subdued and negated Carlton's Blackness by calling him a success as he moved up the ladder, Will's extroverted personality was seen as a failure of the academy's ability to civilize this wild one, no matter what his final SAT score tells us about his actual capacity for learning.*

I didn't fully experience this difference until I went to high school.

In 1996, I entered Xavier High School, a 150-year-old independent Jesuit university-preparatory high school for young men on Manhattan's West Side. I chose Xavier because, of all the Catholic all-boys schools in New York City, it had the best mix of rigorous academics and locale. With a high GPA out of middle school, I made it into Xavier on academic scholarship, without which my mother would have never been able to afford the tuition for such an elite institution. Xavier prides itself on football, rugby, the marching band, and *not* having to take the New York State Regents Exams—a testament to the steep academic climb students must undertake in order to graduate.

---

* In the episode "The Alma Matter," Will gets into Princeton University, Carlton's dream school, just by being himself during an interview. (And scoring in the ninety-first percentile on the SATs.)

It took thirty minutes by bus from the Lower East Side to get to Chelsea, the neighborhood Xavier called home. To some that might sound like a long commute, but I was able to get home at a reasonable hour from extracurricular activities while still getting a slice of life in another neighborhood.

Xavier High School at the time was 78 percent white, with a relatively even distribution of Asians, Latinos, and Blacks—so it was a bit of a culture shock. Before I arrived at Xavier, my contact with white people had primarily been in the form of police officers, priests, teachers . . . and more police officers. The remaining white people on my radar wore spandex pants and ripped their shirts off in steroid-induced rages like Hulk Hogan or Randy "Macho Man" Savage, played dad to two adopted Black kids like Phil Drummond, or played on the 1992 Olympic Dream Team (the only one that counts!) like John Stockton and Chris Mullin. White people felt so omnipresent in the culture that surrounded me, I could easily imagine how the average white person lived. On the other hand, it was impossible to imagine the average white person knowing how I lived, outside of whatever rap videos and movies like *Boyz n the Hood* told them.

The first CD (remember those?) I ever bought was Janet Jackson's *Design of a Decade*. My immediate second: Alanis Morissette's *Jagged Little Pill*. I delved into alternative rock and electronic music partly as a way of shielding my mom and God from knowing that I thoroughly enjoyed the Notorious B.I.G.'s "Big Poppa" and Dr. Dre's "Let Me Ride," with all the "bullshits" and "chronic" mentions unfiltered. I grew up on Daisy Fuentes and MTV's *Headbangers Ball*, and when my family moved to the projects, cable access pulled Guns n' Roses and Snoop Doggy Dogg into my house. Conflicted and overwhelmed by the range of pop culture thrown in my direction, I dabbled in as much as possible. Perhaps I didn't want to feel limited in my conversations, but it had the effect of displacing me from many of the groups I had thought I fit into. My discomfort with my own skin didn't help, and now I would go to a school populated by with boys with considerable economic, intellectual, and physical swagger.

Nevertheless, in my first couple of years of high school, I asserted myself as a confident student determined to make his mark out of the gate. I enrolled in all the honors classes I could, took up a few clubs, and maintained a good enough average for first and second honors each quarter. In my first year, my grades were in the top 10 percent of my class, right where I felt I belonged. But I also committed to a self-taught crash course in extreme code-switching. At Nativity, I had white teachers who had made efforts to build bridges between their world and ours. Some of them, like my seventh-grade English teacher Ms. Miranda, had engaged with our community for years, showing a clear sense of empathy as well as high expectations for her students. Others, like my eighth-grade math and science teacher Mr. Murphy, were young enough to acclimate to our music and style, dropping pop culture and basketball references into their teaching.

Xavier was different.

There I was most at home in the lunchroom, surrounded by fellow Nativity alumni. I fell back into my street slang as we complained about our teachers. My friends and I tried our best to stick together, but only saw each other outside class and after school, when we would take the F train downtown to Nativity to play three-on-three basketball almost every afternoon until five. On the way home we griped more about our teachers, but we shared a deep-seated responsibility to succeed. We wouldn't let each other drop out. The instruction we received at Nativity rang in our ears, as if Father Jack himself was telling us, "If you can climb the tallest mountains in New York State, you can handle this, right?"

Yes, Father.

In my honors and advanced classes, I toned down the "hood" in me, mimicking instead the academic language of my teachers and fellow students. For every teacher who nominated me for an award or peer who helped me with my math homework, there

were others who refused to negotiate their airs for a pudgy Black
kid they thought was trying to act white. When we discussed poetry
or contemporary music in class, kids would say things like, "José,
can you rap some Ma$e for us?" Boys will always rib each other,
but prompting the Black kid to rap didn't sit well with me. Even if
I did have the 1997–99 Bad Boy Records catalogue memorized, I
didn't see myself as anyone's urban jukebox. In everyone else's eyes
it looked innocent, so, as with many microaggressions, I left it alone.

Microaggressions—those little, ostensibly innocent actions
that highlight a person's privilege or lack thereof—are a concept
I wish I'd had at my disposal back then. We are taught to think of
racism as looking like pointy white hoods, but microaggressions
are much more common and complex. At Xavier, we embraced
the championship-winning Yankees as a symbol of New York
pride and multiculturalism. The team included an Italian-Cajun
lefty (Andy Pettitte), a Cuban defector (Orlando Hernández), an
all-boys-Jesuit-school wizard (David Cone), a collection of field-
ers and pitchers from all over Latin America (Mariano Rivera,
Ramiro Mendoza, Tino Martinez, Jorge Posada), and a biracial
kid from Kalamazoo (Derek Jeter), led by Italian manager Joe
Torre. When the Yankees won a championship, Xavier celebrated
with dress-down days and a day off so we could get to the parade.
Baseball made race relations look easy.

At the same time, the kids of color—and some white students—
had not-so-secret discussions that highlighted the racial divisions
that ran through our school. One example: the annual debate over
whether the Black kid or the white kid deserved a spot on the
school basketball team. The team only had twelve spots and there
were at least fifty boys willing to do running drills, push-ups, and
whatever else the coaches asked to get on the team. Every fall, we'd
speculate who would make it based on what we saw in gym class.
Our football and rugby teams always got citywide and nationwide
recognition, while the basketball teams, skilled as they were, simply
couldn't hang with the likes of Rice or La Salle.

Thus, in our school, any discussion about who was "nice" in ball had a racial component. The ball teams we saw on TV were predominantly Black with white coaches. Xavier's basketball team looked like the coaches didn't want to let go of their *Hoosiers* fantasies. We'd laugh, but when the roster came out for the basketball team and the twelfth man was white, the debates got fierce. "How is he on the team when half of the Black kids we saw on the practice court are better than dude?!" Those not-so-secret lunch conversations became a roar, with one table of mostly Black kids shaking their heads for the whole lunch period.

When this happened during my senior year, the tension got so bad that students organized a spontaneous five-on-five. One team had the starters from the varsity basketball team. The other was made up of the best players who hadn't made the squad. It was a Black and white affair. One coach I ran into leaving the gym clearly didn't know how to address it. How could he?

As the bell sounded, the juniors and seniors watching the game had broken up into two sides: the Italian and Irish students versus the students of color. No one fought, but each cheered their "side" on. No one spoke about it afterward. No one knew the actual score. No one won.

These tensions existed among the faculty, too. For every Mass we had together as a community, we had a Black or Latino teacher who felt slighted or left abruptly for reasons I didn't fully understand. Mr. Caesar, an assistant principal my freshman year, was one of the handful of Black men in the school. He stood at six foot three, with a suit and tie, rattling the halls with his sonorous tones. An alum himself, Mr. Caesar had everyone's respect; even his smile demanded every student's attention. When our headmaster became the president of Xavier High School, we all assumed Mr. Caesar would become the new headmaster. Instead, Father Ciancimino took over, with the higher-ups explaining that they wanted to reserve the headmaster position for an ordained priest. As the news spread at lunch, the kids of color snickered. The "we wanted a priest" argument seemed credible, yet it just didn't feel right. It felt even worse when Mr. Caesar left for another school the next year.

Father C, as we called him, was a good headmaster. What I most admired about him was his willingness to sit with the Nativity boys at lunch. He had heard about us from Father Jack, and at first his biweekly five-minute visits to our table unnerved us. By then I had gained a reputation for my good grades—but also my constant lateness. Without his grace, I might have lost my scholarship after my grades dipped. He also rounded up funds for me and my friends to get our graduation rings, an act of generosity that only further complicated my relationship with Xavier as a school. How could I negotiate the pride and humility I felt about so many of the experiences I had there with the inner racial turmoil playing out with me, to me, around me?

Every year, it felt like one of my Black or Latino classmates left for La Salle Academy or Cardinal Hayes High School, schools with reputations for more people of color on their rolls. I didn't have language for it, but my awareness of privilege was becoming more palpable than the funk emanating from our lockers on gym day.

During Christmas break my junior year, one of my aunts died of leukemia and it devastated my family for the rest of that holiday. After I came back to school, a priest I confided in prayed for my family and me. A few days later, our guidance counselor rounded a group of us together and asked us to share something about our winter breaks. Everyone shared something mundane: the foods they ate, the places they traveled, the families sharing gifts around a pine tree. When it was my turn, in a rare moment of candor, I confided that my aunt had died, so my Christmas break had been spent mostly in mourning. The guidance counselor looked at me, eyes as blank as a new sheet of loose-leaf, and said, "Okay, so anyway . . ."

I imagined the round dinner tables of my classmates, turkey in the middle, Christmas lights glistening above the head of the table, grinning, sharing jokes, calibrating each other's experiences with others like them. I already understood my experiences as "different," my isolation clear from the moment the guidance counselor anticipated a "different" response. The tragedy that beset my family may have surprised everyone in that session, but the ambivalent response felt prepared, more an institutional response to kids of color than a personal misunderstanding on the counselor's part. Otherwise, I might have been asked, "Can we meet in private after this?," which is what guidance counselors generally get trained to do for their children.

I learned how to parse the things I couldn't control from the things I could, but this tension kept tugging at my collar. It just never pulled me to the point of anger until my junior year, when I took English 11 Honors. As usual, I was one of just two kids of color in the class. (The other kid of color was one of the few Black student athletes we wanted representing us on the basketball team.) The teacher was legendary. He had more than a half-century of teaching under his belt and was revered for his intellect and mastery of his subject. It was rumored that he kept every single paper from every student he'd ever had in a secret room upstairs, just to make sure no one copied from anyone else. Everyone I ever asked had nothing but high praise for him, so getting that 11H tag on my schedule felt like a privilege.

During the year I spent in his class, I found myself constantly wondering when I would make my breakthrough. Paper after paper, no matter how much time and care I invested, the highest grade I received was an eighty-five. My classmates got their papers back littered with red marks, just like mine, yet they all received consistent scores of ninety or higher.

Patiently waiting for a chance to prove my mettle, I told myself repeatedly that my own lack of intellectual fortitude had led to my low grades my first semester. After my twelfth straight eighty-something score on a paper, I went back to Nativity to visit Father Jack and ask him what I could do. He suggested I speak to the teacher. The next morning, I tried to approach him before class, but he waved me off and sent me to my seat. Fair enough. I was used to waiting for the things I wanted. I just couldn't wash my mouth of the sour taste of another eight-five on another paper. I sat there seething, waiting my turn to prove him wrong.

A few weeks later, we were preparing for another exam when the teacher asked me to read a question aloud. I read it as clearly as possible. He asked me what the answer was. I said "D." Everyone in the class nodded. He said, "What?" I said, "D." Everyone looked at the teacher again. He said, "What? I didn't hear that." I yelled, "D!" startling my classmates. The teacher just waved a hand at me and said, "Well you don't know anything, so I'll move on. Tom, how about you?"

Tom, sitting next to me, said, "D."

"Good answer, that's the right answer. Good job, there."

My eyes dropped lower than my jaw. The rest of the class laughed nervously. I almost couldn't believe it. I didn't have the vocabulary at the time to discuss the incident, or the culmination of other experiences that hinted at racial bias, but it was clear to me that some people I had once assumed had my best interests at heart did not. Up to that point, "acting white" had been a means of survival, assuring that people couldn't deny me access to schooling or anything else because of their perceptions when I reflected their speech patterns, their interests, and their version of history. This teacher had negotiated my grades with my skin already.

After that incident, my optimism for racial harmony, at least in high school, was dashed. By that time, I had played the trombone at the Columbus Day Parade, taken on the role of Superman at the last minute for the freshman play, fundraised for the David Cone Foundation, and volunteered in the pediatric unit at New York–Presbyterian Hospital. I had been included in the *Who's Who Among American High School Students* collection. Yet I still found myself wondering who the hell I thought I was.

In my senior-year history class, we were assigned a paper on the topic of our choosing. I chose slavery and picked up Chinua Achebe's *Things Fall Apart,* a book I had first bought in sixth grade at a library book sale. (After one of my teachers took it, lost it, and brought another—read: less valuable—edition of the book for me, I had lost interest in reading it.) In retrospect, I "blacked up" the paper on purpose. I don't recall the title, but I know I threw in slavery and white people a few times for good measure. In one of the few things I remember from the thesis, I dismissively proclaimed that, even as some of us get dressed up in uniform, white people still look at us the way slavemasters looked at slaves.

A few days later, my history teacher handed back everyone's paper but mine and whispered to me, "Can I see you after class?" I knew I had "stepped in it." He pulled me aside after class and told me that my paper was racist drivel and I should take everything back. Or else. I certainly didn't want to hurt anyone's feelings, even though I probably needed to mature in my own understanding of race. Yet I didn't feel anything either Achebe or I had said was untrue.

Still, I recanted it all, with regret and resentment simmering in my belly.

That same year, the teacher who had humiliated me in class my junior year passed away and Xavier students were invited to attend a special open-casket service. When it was my turn to pray in front of his casket, I couldn't bear it; I sat out in the dimly lit hallway and cried. Most people assumed I was upset at his death—and to a certain extent I was. Yet I was more upset at the hurt and hate he let seep into my heart. That he would die before I got to tell him about himself bothered me more than anything else.

In those moments of despair, one of my saving graces came while singing for the choir my junior and senior years. Ms. Kittany, with whom I still keep in touch to this day, unlocked a voice that I didn't know I had. She was one of the few teachers in the building who got it. I didn't have much of an interest in singing until I got cast in the school musical, *South Pacific*, in 1997. When she first invited me to sing for her choir after the musical, I replied, "Why would you want to do that to your choir?" I accepted anyway, despite my trepidation about performing. Every Mass felt like an assessment of my progress, and I probably failed more times than passed. I went from singing as part of the choir to taking the role of cantor. Some people doubted my voice, saying that it cracked. It did, which made my soul sore for a week.

But Ms. Kittany just worked harder with me, waiting patiently for her faith to be rewarded. During my last Mass before graduation, she just looked at me and signaled to the mic. I don't remember much besides her crying as the bass took over my voice box. As she walked away from me, trying to wipe her tears, I looked at the book of canticles in front of me and wondered whether I'd ever have a chance to use my voice this well again, even if I wasn't going to sing with it. I never had her as one of my core subject teachers, but what she taught me about the power of my voice was one of the most important lessons I took away from my experience at Xavier High School.

Praise be to God.

IT'S NOT ABOUT A SALARY

Before college, I only had one Black male teacher. His name was Mr. Wingate and he taught Computer Applications in twelfth grade. He didn't teach me anything profound, since Microsoft products don't lend themselves to intellectual depth or deep revelations, but he made an impression. He caught hell for his bowties and diction, speaking too properly and taking himself rather seriously. His speech seemed to be a mockery of what the students thought was English.

If I've done the math correctly, out of the fifty or so teachers I've had in my lifetime, only two or three of them were men of Black or Latino descent. For someone who was born and raised in New York City, that's staggering.

You're allowed to wonder why that's so important. After all, teachers of all races, backgrounds, sexes, and ages have proven effective educators of urban youth.

I love that so many white people care about the plight of Black and Latino students that they're open to working in the neighborhoods they're in. Many of my white teachers were excellent. I get that there needs to be a diversity of experiences; our students have to survive in the same world as everyone else. A small part of me also thinks: Who better to teach urban youth the tools needed to survive in a predominantly white country than . . . white people?

But I'd be lying if I told you I wasn't disturbed by the lack of representation of Black or Latino males as teachers. Some work as

51

principals, school aides, and staff, and others are third-party vendors, education lawyers, and professors in institutions of higher education. Effective (and ineffective) teachers often leave the classroom in favor of these occupations; while plenty of men do great work in administration, too many men use it as a means of staying in education without grounding themselves in the educational practice of the classroom.

Because more than 80 percent of the nation's teachers are women, our society also views teaching as "women's work"—a category that often leads to demeaning and obtuse ways of dismissing teachers' contributions. This dynamic compounds the already existing problem of society talking down to educators in our schools. Too many people don't see the need to pay teachers well or to ensure they have proper working conditions because they see us as caretakers, not professionals. Where male-dominated professions like computer science or medicine get respect, the teaching profession still has to combat patriarchy.

The fact that so many people view teaching as a second-class profession speaks volumes about our society's values. Plenty of men talk favorably about teachers, but when asked if they'd ever be teachers themselves, they respond, "I don't have the patience," and "You guys don't get paid enough." In our society, money means stature, whether we value the person who holds the position or not. It's not just coming from this generation, either. My mom, whom I love dearly, on occasion wonders aloud why, with all the stress and duress I endure as a teacher, I would put up with this mess when I could make 150 percent more as a computer programmer.

There are those who have left the profession because it's really easy to get jaded about the school system *and* the human experience. I don't know any fellow Black or Latino male (or female) teachers who think that every student in their school is getting properly served by this school system. Some conclude that the system is hopeless. Others say, "We'll continue to fight." The latter are crucial: When our students *see* more Black or Latino sports figures populating a multimillion-dollar court or field and yet only one Black or Latino teacher in their whole grade, or two or three in their whole school, then they're probably less inspired to take teaching seriously. It's why, for a generation, rappers like Rakim and KRS-One kept talking about teaching: because they didn't feel educated in the classroom. That's why, when we see a crowd gathered around a wild, ranting man in Harlem, we should listen more closely to why his message resonates with the crowd than to the sensationalism of his rhetoric.

History helps explain the lack of male Black or Latino teachers, too. It was Mississippi-based teacher and National Board of Professional Teaching Standards board member Renee Moore who first told me the extraordinary story of how Black teachers in the South (especially males) were systematically dismissed or ostracized from their positions after the *Brown v. Board of Education* decision, in anticipation of integrated public schools. Shortly thereafter, school boards removed Black educators in droves and replaced them with brand-new, mostly white teachers. Nowadays, people rarely point out the racial undertones of replacing a staff who achieved their positions via "traditional" routes with teachers who have completed a prestigious alternative certification program that mainly solicits people from the most exclusive colleges and the upper echelons of their college classes. It is critical that we view the racially disparate impact of today's reform efforts through the lens of institutionalized racism.

Whether I was aware of it or not, Jaime Escalante had stayed in my mind since I was first introduced to his story. I aspired to be just like him. But there was also more to his story.

Soon after his death in 2010, we learned more details about Escalante's relationship with his school administration and how it affected his teaching, in part due to a book by Henry Gradillas, the Garfield High School principal who had seen the value in Escalante's famed accelerated math program. After Gradillas left, the administration that replaced him did not show the same support, which undermined Escalante's ability to help his students pass the same AP exam. He was also, in a way, the victim of his own success: more students flocked to his class than he could handle, along with too many special visitors, presidents and movie stars among them, generating jealousy from his fellow teachers in the process. The number of students taking AP Calculus at Garfield High today averages somewhere in the teens, nowhere near the level that Escalante and those who supported him achieved. Nevertheless, Escalante did amazing things during his time as the head of the math department at Garfield High School. Most importantly, whole communities felt a kinship with him. His persona carried that program and eventually inspired many others to get into teaching—including me.

I can't always pinpoint what makes me, or any man of color, any different from other teachers of different backgrounds, but here are some things I've learned:

- The Black/Latino male students respond more readily to me.
- The girls in my class are more willing to share their experiences with me and often look to me to as a role model or father figure.
- The people in my class may act like they hate me temporarily after I've scolded them about something, but they know I have their best interests at heart.
- They ask me about what it was like when I was growing up, because they know my experiences mirror theirs.
- Some of them have considered becoming teachers because of me.
- Many teachers of color have seen firsthand what might happen if their children *don't* get a good teacher.

It is clearly important for my students to see an authority figure who looks like them, understands what they're going through, challenges them, and provides a model for how to act.

The year after Escalante's passing, in 2011, I had the privilege of attending an event in Tarrytown, New York, held by the organization Today's Students Tomorrow's Teachers. The program was founded by Dr. Bettye Perkins to encourage more teachers of color to enter the profession through an eight-year program that provides mentorship through high school and half to full college tuition scholarships; all they have to do is get their certifications and become teachers. I wish such a group had existed when I first came into my own, but I'm excited that people like me have this opportunity now. I was invited to share a few remarks, which I titled "It's Not About A Salary, It's All About Reality," a quote from KRS-One's classic "My Philosophy."

> Who gets weaker? The king or the teacher?
> It's not about a salary; it's all about reality
> Teachers teach and do the world good
> Kings just rule and most are never understood

I shared these lines to encourage the attendees to consider the ways educators don't merely expect to be followed but inspire students to think for themselves. I also gave a few points by way of advice: for example, "Sample the best teachers from your past, but make your own story."

In my first month of teaching, I told them, I had this crazy idea that I would transform my students' lives and that they would change for me the way Jaime Escalante's did in *Stand and Deliver*. They didn't. But that first class was probably my favorite, and the one from which I learned the most.

One time, we did a lesson on percentages. I wrote my lesson using the technical aspects of finding percentages. As I began to teach it and see the bored look on my students' faces, I had an idea. I wrote the word "percent" out and asked my kids, "Does anyone recognize a word in here?"

"Cent!"

I said, "Oh good! Now, has anyone ever heard of the word somewhere else, even in Spanish?"

Kids jumped out of their seats, they were so excited to answer.

A few kids shouted, "Ooh! Ooh! *Centavo!*"

"So what does *centavo* mean?"

"A penny!"

"And how many pennies do you need to get a dollar again?"

"A hundred!"

"So when we say *percent* we mean we're comparing one thing out of a possible hundred."

"OOHHHHH!!"

That piece of my lesson took about ten minutes more than I planned for, I explained. But it also made a huge difference. Teachers who can relate to their students on a cultural level can reach their students in important ways.

I'm not saying people from other cultures can't help us, but every student of color could use a role model. If their role model just happens to be the teacher in front of them, that's perfect.

We have high expectations for the children sitting in front of us because we were once them. We can tell the difference between a kid not knowing how to add fractions and not knowing how to say the word "fraction," because many of us were once English language learners. We don't take "Yo, what up, teacher?" or "Hey, miss!" to be a sign of illiteracy, but a sign that they want to connect with us as human beings. Our importance as teachers of color stems from this dire need for kids of all races and backgrounds to see people of color as multidimensional and intelligent people, different in culture but the same in capability and humanity.

We're also the ones who can make relevant connections that keep our students engaged in the work. In order to be twenty-first-century teachers, we're no longer going to be the MCs. Sometimes we'll be the DJs and sometimes the producers. Yet we'll always know the beat, the boom-bap that drove you and me to teach. It's the same one that will inspire many others as well.

It's not about a salary; it's all about reality.

THE ANSWER

Mom asks me tons of questions, yet this is the one I can't dodge, old as I am.

"Why did you want to teach, anyway?"

More accurately, my mom said, "¿Y por qué tu cogiste ese tema de informática si tu ibas a enseñar, mi hijo? ¡Eso fue puro gasto!"*

Or something like that.

Dominican moms can be so reassuring.

In my household, education was a binary code: either you made it all the way through twelve years of school, leading directly into college, or you failed at life. Our relatives throughout New York sold drugs, drove livery cabs, or owned bodegas, locking them into their respective neighborhoods for as long as the job demanded. Children on the block dreamt of being the next Jordan at a time when a guy shot another guy a few blocks from our school for his pair of Jordans. Or they sought to model themselves after 2Pac and Biggie—instant success stories until Mr. Shakur and Mr. Wallace were shot at the tender ages of twenty-five and twenty-four, respectively. They also loved the movie *Scarface*, but never mention his fatal shooting at the hands of an unnamed assailant.

Whose world is this?

It's true that I had once set out to be a computer programmer. I'd gotten my hands on a fair amount of technology growing up in

---

* Loosely translated: "Why did you pick that computer science major if you were going to teach anyway, my son? That was a pure waste!"

the late eighties and early nineties. I had seen video games evolve from a black screen featuring a pixel moving from left to right to little cartoon plumbers flying across three-dimensional kaleidoscopic landscapes. My schools' computer labs came equipped with Apple models; Windows-based personal computers became cheaper options for people in poverty. I'd watch CNET's daily show with John C. Dvorak on the Sci-Fi Channel as religiously as I watched the first animated X-Men series on FOX. By the time I was sixteen, my mind was fixed on the idea that I would be a computer programmer.

Nothing could stop me.

Not that people tried. In fact, most of my friends and loved ones thought the sky was the limit for me. My immediate family had envisioned me becoming a doctor, a lawyer, or any profession that would push me (and us) into the upper middle class. I didn't have role models to follow or an official mentor to tell me to follow my computer-programming dream. I didn't know about the lack of Black or Latino computer scientists, nor did I think to investigate. The teachers who put a computer in front of me all had different upbringings, including a Jewish lady in my elementary school, a Puerto Rican brother at my local Boys Club on the corner of Pitt and Houston Streets,* an Italian lady who taught me the fine details of typing in Microsoft Word my junior year of high school, and a Black man with a festive bow tie in high school. But no one was in a position to help me understand the prerequisites. As long as I repeated "computer science" to myself, I figured everything would work itself out.

I applied to Syracuse University, fully intending to graduate with a degree in computer science. Its financial aid program was amazing, the school environment captured me, and my first impression of the staff was positive. But during my first programming class, my teacher bored me so much I filled my notebook half with

---

* It almost became the Boys and Girls Club in the early 2000s but was eventually sold off to Common Ground, a nonprofit housing and community development organization.

notes and half with doodles. I jotted messages in C and Java next to fanciful patterned boxes and depictions of people I knew; I probably learned more from the doodles than the notes. My professor taught with an overhead projector and the darkness of the room made me want to nap.

My math classes didn't go much better: I got lost in the hundred–to-one student/teacher ratio and my eyes glazed over regardless of whether I sat in the back or the middle of the dimly lit auditorium. I struggled with a C average in those classes, the whole time thinking, "I can teach this better. Much better." I usually took a nap shortly after that thought.

Outside of class, the endless nights in the computer lab staring at brackets, commas, and error messages felt like a kick between the eyes. I must have consumed seventy bags of peanut M&Ms over the course of the semester, trying to sort through problems that took the average programmer five minutes. My roommate Richard Duck, also a fellow Black computer science candidate, said to me, "José, our lives could end up looking like *Office Space*." He laughed. I shrugged because I'd never seen this movie. He made me watch it.

Whoa.

From then on I stared at my coding partners, thinking, "Are we going to end up throwing a printer out the office and beating it up with bats, wondering where our lives went wrong? Will I ever get my stapler back? Should I even lend it out to begin with?"

◆

My dissatisfaction with my major only increased when I got involved in extracurricular activities and found them more fulfilling than my coursework. It was my first real introduction to cultural organizations, courtesy of a few young ladies in La LUCHA (Latino Undergraduates Creating History in America). As small as their meetings were—just ten to fifteen people—they fed me a history

I had never been motivated to look for myself. Names like César Chávez and Ernesto "Che" Guevara resonated for reasons I couldn't fully understand. Outside of Martin Luther King Jr. and Rosa Parks, I didn't know much about my own history. Until that point, even the most well-intentioned adults had never introduced me to these resources, which would have done so much for my self-knowledge. This had much to do with where I grew up; besides reading books like Achebe's *Things Fall Apart* and *Roll of Thunder, Hear My Cry* by Mildred Taylor, I don't remember having access to the same cultural education as my colleagues from middle-class Black families. This was not the failing of my few Black and Latino teachers as much as of the curriculum we were taught. From kindergarten through high school, our schooling was designed to cover a "normative" set of educational standards and narratives that did not allow much room to deviate to teaching my own culture or history.

Joining the Student African American Society had a similar effect on me. Older students in the group mentored me and showed me what it meant to be an activist. The group invited speakers like Bobby Seale, Amiri Baraka, and Angela Davis, who inspired and solidified a desire in me to adopt a more radical, bandana-wearing persona. Poet Sonia Sanchez once wrote in my old notepad, "Write new words"—encouraging the younger generation to stop trying to be the next MLK, the next Malcolm, the next Rosa, and be the first of their own kind. She also challenged us to stop cursing for a month. I was much better at the first suggestion.

I discussed the digital divide with the local chapter of the National Society of Black Engineers and the overt racism of the local Denny's with Asian Students in America. This gave me a language for how to discuss my own ongoing experiences, something my computer science curriculum just couldn't do. I dug up the histories of the student organizations along with the writing of Malcolm X, Howard Zinn, Dolores Huerta, and Carter G. Woodson. I studied them during my off-hours, quietly building up my self-esteem and sense of empowerment as a potential leader. By the time I became

La LUCHA's education chair, I was ready to get into those meetings and kick some butt. I taught workshops on César Chávez, mentored students who approached me, and familiarized myself with the administrators. While computer science was my academic major, Black and Latino cultural studies became my life's focus. I was determined to return to my community and represent.

In my senior year, La LUCHA and the Office of Multicultural Affairs brought Edward James Olmos himself to campus. He was every bit the charismatic person we expected based on his performance as Jamie Escalante in *Stand and Deliver*, the very image of the teacher I wanted to emulate. Escalante had not decided to "move up" (read: out) to another school in favor of more privileged students; he kept pushing his program for the underprivileged, the *vagabundos*, the ones society didn't see as calculus students.

Olmos started his lecture with the statement, "Acting is the art of being." That was the moment I realized that everything I wanted to be could only emerge through the things I did (and didn't do). Olmos had suddenly planted a fork in the middle of the road ahead of me. I could continue struggling with programming, maybe design video games or manage a computer project, start off with a 60K salary, and look at code all day. Or I could become a teacher. In New York, the latter would mean a starting salary of 40K, ninety "clients" off the bat, substandard working conditions, and a chance to pay back all the good fortune I had received from my seventeen years of schooling.

I chose teaching.

I did stick with my computer science major and graduated with a bachelor of science in 2004. I told everyone that I would fall back on teaching in case I couldn't find my dream job—even as I began to consider trading in my new mortarboard for a chalkboard.

Part Two

THE POST-TFA ASSESSMENT

"Congratulations, you've been accepted into Teach for America!"

Roar. Fist pump. Quick and extended leaps into the air. Maybe a little run around my dorm room with a piece of paper and a rebel yell of "I'm the greatest" at everyone I saw.

That's exactly how I fantasized about what I saw as my inevitable acceptance into TFA, naively believing I had aced my interview with the organization.

Instead, I got rejected. In retrospect, based on the criteria at the time, I probably wouldn't have hired me either.

The TFA hiring process takes candidates like me through a series of assessments to see if we have the mettle to join its ranks. Applicants must detail everything from their grades to why they want to enter the classroom. Once I got through the initial round, I was invited to a group interview, where I was given more information about TFA and the requirements for getting into the program. Then we each had to teach a lesson in front of a mock class consisting of the other interviewees and the interview team. Afterward, the team interviewed us individually, throwing in a few softball questions ("Why do you want to teach?" "What is your teaching philosophy?") to see how we would respond.

During this second round, I knew my undoing was nigh. My GPA was just below a 3.0, because computer science majors can't have nice things. I didn't prepare for the interview well; I found out that Googling lesson plans only brings up boring text files and, well,

I wanted something authentic. In the middle of ironing my suit, chasing down a recommendation letter from a mentor I'd asked only two days prior, and getting my missing assignments from my early class, I already looked like I had run twenty laps around campus, collared shirt and tie notwithstanding. My lesson plan on exponents fell flat with the fifteen or so other applicants, who knew this material rather well. But I felt so positive about my answers to the interview questions that I hoped they would forget my GPA, my weird lesson plan, and my clammy hands and drenched forehead.

The present me has smacked up the twenty-two-year-old me a few times for this.

A couple of weeks later, I got my rejection letter in my dorm mailbox. I walked around campus stunned, wondering how I could possibly have messed this up. A couple of my friends did get in; they just shook their heads after I told them my news. The education chair of La LUCHA couldn't get a teaching job? I kept my mouth shut with a few of my other friends, but I drank my funk away at a couple of local bars.

As I struggled to finish my senior year at Syracuse, I had a hard time juggling my job as a campus security supervisor with my schoolwork. As a residence security aide and then a supervisor, I had the task of monitoring access to one of nine residence halls throughout the campus, a job I took to make sure my family didn't have to send me money they didn't have. Pulling graveyard shifts didn't lend itself to learning database programming or Calc 3 at nine in the morning. The summer before I finally graduated, as I tried to complete a physics class, I simply couldn't balance my job with academics. I was effectively let go from a job that had named me Employee of the Month not long before.

Humble pie: served.

The jobs didn't come flooding in once I got my degree. I volunteered with Syracuse University's admissions office in New York City and created its Latino Alumni Network, which now boasts more than six hundred official members. But none of this helped on the job front. I sent my CV to every single lead I could find. I had ten different résumés for ninety different jobs, thirty-five different leads, and not a single job to my name. I went to a temp agency and thought I'd aced that process, too; I guess typing seventy words per minute made me overqualified.

By then, I had made my first foray into the world of blogging. At the end of my senior year I set up an anonymous Xanga site, mainly to keep up with friends, but ended up spending a lot of time ranting about then-president George W. Bush. This didn't particularly help my bank account. I attended some community meetings and antiwar protests in Union Square, but the household bills still piled up higher than my mom alone could reach. My cousin, who was serving in the Armed Forces, suggested I join the army. My parents, who didn't want to hear of any Dominican man in their midst without a job, told me to try it out.

Another day, another conscientious objection. Like Muhammad Ali, except without the athletic build, the championship belts, or the support of millions of adoring fans.

In other words, nothing like Muhammad Ali.

Broke and living in my mother's house, I found that days of calling and emailing potential employers did not pay off. Most of my Syracuse connections bore no fruit. It was a depressing period that made me question my idea of college as a whole. If it was all about career readiness, then why did I not have a career? What was I missing? This period finally climaxed when I got into a heated discussion with my mother about paying bills that December. I was a 240-pound sack of unemployed, and my mom had tolerated it for months with little complaint. But her patience had frayed and I was getting desperate—never good chemicals in an already combustible relationship.

I remembered a high-school incident with a young lady at McDonald's, back when my boys and I hung out there after school. My ignorant self and a friend, Alex, were cracking jokes with her when I blurted out, "Well, at least I don't work at a McDonald's!"

My friend and I laughed; she didn't. Flushed, she retorted, "Well, with this job, I get to make sure there's food on the table." I hope I apologized, but I don't think I did.

I've had better moments.

A few nights after that flashback, Alex logged on to AOL Instant Messenger. Employed and happy in Maryland, he laughed unmercifully at my expense. My only comeback was reminding him that he was an asshole. Too easy.

After we stopped taking shots at each other, I told him, "Listen, I'm so desperate, I'll even take the job you had a couple of years ago."

"Wait, what? You mean that job I got from my father a few years back?"

"Yes."

"You mean the job where they only paid me eleven dollars an hour?"

"That one."

"Dude, I hated that job. It was a pain in the ass."

"I'll take it. Just hook it up for me."

"You're sure? I mean, that job sucked!"

"Yes! I'll take it. Anything to get off my ass and get back to work!"

"All right, simmer down now." Alex had a thing for sprinkling salt on open and sore wounds. "I'll call them in the morning."

"*Yes!*"

A month later I had the interview. The job was with an educational research firm, doing data entry. I found out I would be paid less as a college graduate (ten dollars an hour) than my friend had earned as a high-school senior ($11.45 an hour). I picked up four hours a day initially, but, within a month, earned enough trust to be assigned the full forty hours a week I needed to help my mother out with rent and get a decent pair of shoes in the process.

In the back of my mind, I still wanted to teach, so I decided to apply for the NYC Teaching Fellows (NYCTF) program, despite the disappointing experience I'd had with TFA. I saw the ads on the F train and said, "This is it." NYCTF felt like the best way into the profession at a time when school districts had made teaching more difficult to get into (contrary to what many education reformers tell the general public). In many ways, the online application was similar to TFA's. Statements, references, and GPA all mattered. When I typed in my final GPA, a notch under 3.0, a warning label appeared on the screen along with a text box asking me to explain why I had such a low GPA.

I think I just wrote: "Computer science."

In the meantime, at work, I accomplished every task that fell onto my desk before it was due. I even stayed longer on Fridays. Copies to be made? *Yes, ma'am.* Deliveries to Brooklyn? *Right away, ma'am.* Decode this PDF because we can't convert it cleanly? *Absolutely, ma'am.* One day my manager asked me if I would ever consider another job. I said teaching. She said, "Cool, me too." We sat there for a minute, just chatting up what we might do if we became teachers.

If.

My manager was pregnant at the time; eventually, she asked me to handle her duties while she went on maternity leave. On a Friday in May, she said, "José, I'm coming back on Monday to train you on some of the other stuff I haven't let you do." That day never came, though: around 8:30 that Monday morning her water broke, so I inherited her work without knowing exactly what I was doing.

At 9:30, I received a phone call from one of the upper-level managers. "José, we need you to get some transcription done."

"Transcription?"

The first thing I did was to look it up on Dictionary.com, the receiver cradled on the left side of my neck. Before I could really get it, the lady on the other end of the phone said, "Listen, it's really easy. I'll give you the headphones, the tape, and the cassette player. All you have to do is type out what you hear."

"Umm. I'll do my absolute best, ma'am."

"And if you can't hear something, just fill it in with your best guess."

"Should . . . be . . . easy . . ."

"Good. You have two hours."

"Great!"

I replayed that tape so much, I had accents memorized. If I heard a stutter, I typed out the stutter. If I heard background noises, I typed out the background noises. I finally had something to prove—mostly to myself. I never again took the people who worked in my position for granted.

Just as I was warming up to this desk job, the NYC Teaching Fellows sent me a letter informing me that I had an interview. After breaking out into a Harlem Shake (the original one, of course), I spent a full two weeks preparing for the interview. On a crisp Saturday in March, with a dry-cleaned, white-collared suit, a blue-striped tie, a fresh lesson plan, and a year of hard-earned confidence and humility under my belt, I headed into a big, empty school. Swarms of twenty- to forty-somethings from across the city came in their most professional attire, clicking heels down newly waxed hallways as NYCTF workers pointed people into their assigned rooms.

Like the TFA, the NYCTF asked us to model a lesson in front of other candidates, as well as interviewing with one of their esteemed alumni. This time, however, my lesson plan went off without so much as a stutter. I worked the room, engaged the "students," and tried to get deep into the exponents lesson in the allotted fifteen minutes. I answered questions thoroughly and insightfully, injecting some of my personal philosophy and insights on schooling into my answers. After I left, I wiped my brow once and headed back home for a nice plate of rice and beans. I knew the NYCTF interview represented a door that had squeaked open, and I absolutely would not let it shut on me this time.

The next letter I got said that I had not made it into the program. I tried to accept that maybe I still needed to work as a data entry guy until I got my life right. But two weeks later, NYCTF reconsidered. I sent my reply immediately, accepting the offer with no hesitation.

◆

"José, I'm so happy for you, but I'm really sad to see you go."

My manager, with baby in arm, gave me a hug and pleaded with me to at least stay until a week before my training in June. Almost a year after getting rejected by one alternative certification program, I had to get my mind around the six-week intensive training for the other. Things were different this time around. After graduating from Syracuse, I had spent plenty of time putting my feet up—to the point where I'd almost lost my bearings. This time I wanted to break the habit.

"I'll be here until Friday, for sure, Dannette."

Friday, June 3, 2005, was my last day at that job. Monday, June 6, 2005, was the first day of my new career. No days off.

BLUE MAGIC

I didn't take my first real sip of alcohol until I was twenty-one. My friend Cecilia Durazo has the only evidence—a black-and-white photograph of my eyes bulging, lips hovering over a specially made margarita—as I consider myself a very private person.

My second, third, and fourth drinks came only a few hours later in a dorm, where I kept a shot glass firmly in hand while I danced, danced, danced my hips off. About a month later, my twice-roommate and fellow Engineering and Computer Science grad Howard Henderson introduced me to my first Blue Moon.

"You'll love it, buddy," he said. I swear, white people know the best beers, without question. It came with a perfectly cut orange slice and a napkin, crisp, cold, and ready for consumption. I might have had four that night as we romped around Marshall Street. Blue Moon soon became my favorite beer. But I didn't partake in too much debauchery until well after college. That is, until I started my summer institute training for the NYC Teaching Fellows.

As an alternative certification program, the NYC Teaching Fellows advertises to career-changers and idealists like me who want to become classroom teachers. My NYCTF advisors prided themselves on how many teachers stayed in the program compared to those in other alt-cert programs like Teach for America. As a teaching fellow I got a six-week training period along with graduate courses, an internship at a school in my assigned college's district, and a handful of quick and dirty Department of Education trainings on reporting sexual abuse and handling hazardous materials. As a math fellow, the program required me to come in two weeks early to be assessed and retrained in middle- and high-school math in order to pass the first state math licensing test, the Content Specialty Test. I was anxious that I would get a facsimile of my math teacher from my junior year of high school; instead I got a very confident, very nerdy math instructor who spoke Spanish on occasion. I approved of it all.

In the gray, windowless classrooms of the City College of New York, most of us seemed to regress to our college selves: the nerds sat in the front, the kids who struggled sat in the back, and everyone else sat with people they either wanted to know better or didn't want to know at all. Our instructor began by giving us a diagnostic to see how far back in the material he would have to go to get us up to speed. When I got my first test back, it had so many wrong answers, I could have wrung out the page like a sponge and it would have spilled red all over the table. The kids in the front, who had been working on this sort of math for the last few years, practically aced it. I found myself attentive and annoyed at the same time. But I had to take my defeat with a straight face. The math classes went from eight in the morning to four in the afternoon, with a small lunch break.

I owed myself a Blue Moon here.

Nevertheless, the first two weeks of training went smoothly, considering that only a few weeks before my only intellectual stimulation had come from deciding whether to go to Quiznos or the fast-food Chinese restaurant for lunch. I went from passing the eighth grade to finally understanding SOH-CAH-TOA* and the implications of the related theorems on angle relationships. Geek alert. I whizzed past two math tests and kicked both their asses with one shoe (at least that's what I told my friends at the bar that

---

* For the non-math folk, SOH-CAH-TOA is a way to remember the relationship between the sine, cosine, and tangent of angles in a right triangle.

weekend). Now that the state believed I knew the math content, the next six-week phase would shove me through the pedagogy.

I owed myself at least two Blue Moons here: one for passing the tests and the other for passing the two-week crash course. Obviously.

♦

In addition to the crash course in subjects we were supposed to go on to teach, every teaching fellow was given a summer-school observe-and-teach assignment. Four days a week we helped the main teacher with the class. Eventually, we would have to do lessons on our own. Afterward, we were given an hour and a half to eat lunch and get to our afternoon sessions at our respective colleges.

My summer-school assignment happened to be the same school that had already hired me for the school year: IS 52 in Washington Heights. I took a day off from my data entry job and hopped on the A train. The long ride uptown gave me time to get my thoughts together, look over my résumé, and remember the responses I had given at the Teaching Fellows interview four months before.

In retrospect, the interview should have tipped me off about the school system itself. The hallways felt too quiet and the office workers were stuffy. They directed me to the fourth floor, where the assistant principal shook my hand, looked at my résumé, exclaimed "Syracuse!" and started to tell me about the math curriculum. He barely asked me anything relevant to my actual teaching. I nodded and smiled, unnerved at how easily I had secured my first teaching assignment.

Among the positive experiences at that school, though, was getting to know another fellow, Siobhan. Along with an experienced math teacher, Siobhan and I formed a trio—a collaborative team-teaching situation, before we even understood the concept. It helped that Siobhan and I identified as Afro-Latinos, appealing to both the Black and Latino students in the classroom, whereas the lead teacher was of African descent and couldn't speak Spanish.

One teacher would teach the general class while the other two would watch and translate for the students. Often Siobhan and I would have to reteach the material when our lead teacher went too far above the students' level of understanding.

When it was our turn to teach, we got a chance to help each other and critique each other's work. The lead teacher eventually took only one day out of the four while Siobhan and I split up the topics according to our strengths. It was hard to say whether we did a good job, but we considered ourselves successful.

Stress? I took a drink for every reason under the Blue Moon, but the mental strain of preparing to become a teacher in ninety days was about the best excuse imaginable. I had a drink for every support group–style talk with our cohort, every soporific auditorium training on child abuse and discipline, every kid with cigarette cartons and condoms hanging out of his pockets, and every time I had to fill out tedious paperwork.

I had a drink for every misconception I had about the profession going in, from what we call "special education" to the leadership capabilities of the professors and principals who directly or indirectly affected our work. I had a drink for every classmate I knew wouldn't make it through the program due to a fragile ego, fragile psyche, or fragile heart. (Or through no fault of their own.) I had a drink for my just-graduated-from-Ivy-League classmates who disrupted class because they thought themselves better than the professors with twenty-two years of public-school teaching experience and for the people who came from other careers hoping to do what was best for their students, only to confront a system not designed for their optimism.

I eventually upgraded to rum and Coke, then Long Island iced tea. In retrospect, my switching drinks foreshadowed the many regime changes my school would see over a seven-year period; the five reorganizations of the NYC school system over an eight-year period; the dozens of administrators, supervisors, and so-called "professional developers" who visited my classroom, playing nice but then getting me into trouble with superiors and cronies who had never stepped into a classroom full-time yet told educators how to do their jobs.

I drank to my own insecurities, to the knowledge that "Mister"—not José—would be my first name from now on, to the issues still lingering at home, to the image in the mirror that still resembled pieces of my father. I drank to the mixed blessing of finally landing in a profession that had throbbed in my mind like a hangover the morning after. All in all, I spent two-fifths of my well-earned stipend on a fun and wildly irresponsible set of weekends the summer before I got my first set of students. That left about three-fifths of my money to pay my federal loans, credit-card debt, part of the rent, and the other regular expenditures I had accumulated over the summer.

Three-fifths for any man of color in this country would break his constitution.

As I completed the summer institute, my advisor sat me down for my final interview and said, "I'm really happy for you. When you first started, I thought you'd never make it. I thought you were too idealistic."

I nodded. I should have exposed my realism to him in clearer terms, but the bags under my eyes clearly indicated that my age in reality—years way beyond my revolutions around the sun.

I'll toast to that.

THE HOMEROOM IS A HOME

On the first day of math class as a Teaching Fellow, I looked at the roster. "Fourteen kids," I said to myself. "Hmm." I was nodding in approval when a little girl with glasses looked up at me and said, "You know it's not going to be this size forever, right?" Scarlett was good for reality checks.

Seventh-graders land at the bottom of my theoretical behavior parabola, based on informal surveys of dozens of teachers (and noneducators) across the country. For those not in the know, the parabola works like an upside-down bell curve, starting from kindergarten all the way through senior year of high school. It starts at a good-behavior peak in kindergarten, then drops. Seventh grade is the low point; upon telling people this was the grade I was teaching, many of them cringed, sighed, or just patted me on the back and wished me well. My naïveté got the best of me on that first day of school. Fourteen students and they were all pleasantly quiet and still, nothing like I expected my first day to be.

Day two brought the rush. As my fourteen kids got seated in the first few minutes, a woman walked in with about sixteen more. They talked loudly and clamored for lockers while they got their registration cards changed from 7H4 to 7H3—my class. I stood there waiting for the process to finish, a whole period of math gone. By the end, the administrators had collapsed two seventh-grade classes into one: fourteen students became the congress of thirty known as 7H3. Of the three classes on this floor (7H1, 7H2,

7H3), this was the one hand-engineered to run me through the rigors of teaching in an urban setting.

I got punked before I even received my first Department of Education (DOE) paycheck.

In addition, I was assigned two high-level classes, one in the eighth grade (8A4) and one in the seventh grade (7A4). My advanced classes had better levels of student attendance, higher levels of parent engagement, and uncanny levels of "idiot savants."

But 7H3, for all its academic struggles, had character. And characters. It had the loud and secretly nerdy Sonya and Salome, who I semi-adopted as my school daughters. The mellow cool of Dalido, Felix, and Rafael H. The young maturity of Bianca, Scarlett, and Josh. The dedication and commitment of Yuleisi, Christina, and JP. The giggly gum-chewers Destiny, Jennifer C., and Jennifer L. The extra-quiet Thannya with the extra-talkative Kelly, and the radiant smilers who frequently came late, Ashley and Amber. The mischievous Jonathan O., the excitable Jonathan P., the beanstalk Jonathan S. It had the calamitous Alex, whose job it was to make my job that much harder; the introvert Christopher, who just needed a pat on the back every so often; the quizzical Mahaish, who always had a round of intelligent questions about everything we did; and Shanaya and Whitney, who snickered their way through every conversation.

My students made it really hard to remain detached, and I tried really hard to stay as objective and measured with them as possible. I didn't smile once until December (more on that later). I made them work for their grades on almost everything, and chased them down through their English, science, and social-studies classes. If I saw them in the hallway, I escorted them back to class. I was brutally honest to all of their parents when I called their houses.

One time I kept the kids after school because they kept uttering the N-word. Rosa Parks had died the day before, and I got so furious at hearing the word that I decided to hold a tutorial on why I feel the way I do about it. I shut the door and wrote "nigger" on the blackboard. Silence. "Now, you listen to me. We didn't fight for you to sit here where you can get an opportunity to do better for yourselves and your communities for you to use this language around each other." It's one of the standard diatribes we concerned folk have. I didn't know where it came from, but I'm glad I had it ready to go.

What amazed me was that, soon after, the whole school learned of this lesson. 7H3 spread it. Students slapped each other's shoulders for using the N-word around me. The amount of respect my students showed for me stirred me, even when many of them didn't try as hard as they could academically. They reciprocated my dedication to them twofold.

This relationship with my students from 7H3 made it that much more jarring to see how they related—or didn't—to the English teacher who taught them. His approach was basically the opposite of mine; as the English instructional coach for the building, he went out of his way to show the world that his Columbia University Teachers' College education was superior. In teacher meetings, his holier-than-thou perfectionism rubbed people the wrong way. What hurt him most, though, was his obvious contempt for the kids. He never had to say it, but the students became so in tune with that hate that they would run, scream, and shout to get into my classroom. It got to the point where, once the bell rang, they would bust open his door and run next door to hide under my tables. As a rookie teacher, I just looked at them and said, "Really?"

Around December 2007, a verbal confrontation erupted between Sonya and the teacher, causing the whole class to spill into the hallway. Sonya, the unofficial spokesgirl for the class, burst out of the class, shaking, in tears. When I heard the commotion in the hallway, I asked what had happened. Trying to ascertain a coherent story from twenty-seven screaming teenagers using the words "fuck" and "shit" like punctuation didn't help.

They told me that the teacher had demanded repeatedly that his students get back to work, but they would not cooperate. After several attempts to get them engaged in the lesson, the teacher had started to home in on—the kids used "pick on"—the more rebellious kids in the class. Even with all the noise surrounding him, he had pinpointed Sonya as the ringleader of the commotion. She'd asked him, "What did I do?!" which then started a back-and-forth.

Having heard his interactions with the class through the shared vent between our rooms, I could imagine that he lost his temper and spoke at an unacceptable volume to the girl, who obviously didn't get why he kept losing his cool. Even as a newbie, I sometimes found myself pulling him aside and asking him, indirectly, why he approached the kids with such venom. I tried to befriend him, calming him down when I caught him in the hallway after teaching 7H3. Here I was, struggling with this class, having to tell a teacher with a decade of experience about how he was talking to *my kids*.

I tried to see it from his point of view, too. Perhaps they could have cooperated a bit more with what he was trying to show them or found other ways of making their voices heard. Perhaps they were frustrated with how he taught and how he didn't reach out to them.

Perhaps they'd had enough. Like I had.

Fortunately, one of the assistant principals stepped in and asked me to look after Sonya while she resolved the situation.

I hadn't been taught how to handle these types of situations. And the horror stories of male educators getting into trouble for showing any sort of care for a young student made me hesitant to cross my professional (read: cold) barrier to comfort her. But I sat next to her in front of the coordinator's office in the hallway while she cried her eyes out. She kept saying, "I don't know why, I don't know why . . ." I just sat there. When she had exhausted herself, she put her head on my shoulder. I put my arm around her and let her cry as she long as she wanted.

Twenty minutes passed.

"I think I want to go back to class."

"You sure?"

"Yeah. I think I'm done."

"All right. Cool."

"Thank you."

We walked back to her class. After dropping her off, I sat there in my room and let the walls vibrate, the ringing in my ears nothing more than the quiet that occupied the big room.

I was discovering what people meant when they said teaching was a calling.

I had put so much effort into maintaining my professional mask—a serious face that created a distance between me and everyone else so we could focus on the math. So why had I let Sonya and 7H3 see me with my guard down? I realized that, as much as I kept trying to push them away, I couldn't keep my students from pulling me in, chipping away at the wall I had built. Even if you've never lived these students' lives, how can you *not* find yourself drawn to their personal stories, their emotions, and their struggles to find their identities in a world that steadily widens every time we teach them something new?

◆

The moments after that brushed past like loose-leaf pages in a binder. The surprise birthday party my students threw that I honestly didn't know was coming, the afternoons playing basketball with them in the upstairs gym, the faces we made when different assistant principals came in ("Mr. Vilson, can you tell her to leave us alone, please?"), the times I had to tell boys that there would be other girls waiting for them who wouldn't break their hearts.

There were also times I felt I had let them down. Sometime that April, the students decided to show me the side of themselves they showed their English teacher. I was writing on the blackboard over the sound of incessant talking. A few kids kept bickering even after I asked them to stop. Some students hadn't even taken out their notebooks, and a few others went to their lockers even after I asked them not to. I had come to class that day with every intention of teaching them angle relationships, but the majority of the class had every intention of ignoring my pleas.

After a while, I just decided to finish writing all the lesson notes on the board and let them do what they wanted. They had tuned me out anyway. Then I sat down at my desk and said, "Okay, so if you won't listen, do what you want." I didn't teach. I didn't do anything. I sat there and let them do whatever. A couple of kids took notes, but the majority did exactly what they wanted. They went to their lockers, chatted with their friends, doodled in their notebooks, and didn't mind doing just as they pleased. It was a huge failure of classroom management. But even more, it was a breach in what I thought was a bond of trust between that group and me.

After the class was over, I sat there in utter disgust at what had just happened, rethinking this teaching business. What the hell was I thinking? How could I invest this much in kids who totally disregarded me on a whim? Did I just need to quit and prove my doubters right?

But the pity party was short. *This isn't how it's going to end, dammit.*

That afternoon during homeroom, I sat them all down. Their heads hung in silence. I had them all stand behind their chairs and gave them the story you've read in this chapter.

"You mean to tell me, after everything we've done together up to this point, all the lessons we learned, how you all run to me when you need me, how I call your parents with hopeful comments about your potential, you're gonna do what you all did that last period? Are you kidding? You keep telling me I'm the only teacher who cares about you and *this* is how you're going to act? Then why am I here? If this is how you show you care about your futures, then I'm extremely disappointed in how you demonstrate it. Tomorrow when we come in, we're going to try again and we're going to do it right. If you can't do that, then this is the wrong classroom for you." My voice, so low yet quaking, astonished and shamed them into lining up quietly. I dismissed them from the top of the stairs, standard procedure for the school. I looked away from them as they each said, "See you later." I walked down the hallway, past my other classes. I ran into my assistant principal's office, and interrupted a casual meeting between her and the math coach.

I broke down.

Mrs. Jackie King, the coordinator for the floor, and Ms. Yesenia Michel, the math coach, listened to this young, usually composed gentleman explain his emotional outburst and did their best to empathize. Their words of encouragement ("You're doing great! Why are you worried?") and their shared experiences ("I didn't always know what I was doing in the classroom, either, but you learn over time") meant *everything* in that moment. They knew it was a tough class; sometimes I caught them walking by the classroom to see how I was doing, even as they were preparing to develop their own school in the Bronx. After a long conversation with them, I took the 1 train to one of my graduate classes, ready to spill my guts about the terrible day I just had. Once I did, Indira, who I was still taking classes with, said it was about time. Most of my fellow Fellows said they'd had their breakdowns back in November. (One even had hers right in front of me.)

Mentally drained, I had a hard time concentrating in my night classes. After getting home at 8:30, I said nothing to my mom about the day I had, only that I was tired and not particularly hungry. But I *was*. I was hungry for another day to make up for this horrible day.

The next day, I came back renewed.* I had needed to go through that horrible day, to be pushed to my limits. When I came into the school building that morning, my United Federation of Teachers (UFT) chapter leader spotted me in the hallway as I was

---

* Word to the wise: Always go back the next day. You'll thank me later.

escorting my kids to lunch and said in his burly growl, "Vilson, you're doing a yeoman's job."

"Huh?"

"A yeoman's job."

"What?"

"You're doing a HELLUVA job, Vilson!"

Thanks.

For all the mini-dramas that played out during my first year of teaching, I would never trade that experience for any other. These are the stories I love to tell to friends. These were the kids who inspired me to have my own.

People in my position (along with researchers and experts) like to enforce certain, largely middle-class, values on students who already come with a set of values that work for them. I'm not saying that students don't have misbehavior issues, but people make poor kids' behaviors out to be pathological, as if those who don't misbehave are the exception. Rich kids are seen as well-behaved except for a few spoiled brats. That's an unfortunate stereotype, one that reeks of internalized capitalist oppression. When we assume poor kids behave as they do *just because* of their poverty and not as a manifestation of their *frustration* with poverty, we do an injustice to their humanity.

I know we mean well, but we're missing the mark. We just need to work with what they come with and use it to our advantage. My homeroom doesn't always care to behave well. They're going to interrupt you, yell at you, curse at you, and disrespect you. They're not always going to walk in formation for you, do all your homework, speak in the King's English (although this country did overthrow the monarchy), or listen to your lectures when you speak to them. If your response as an adult is to highlight how much more perfect your culture is compared to theirs, then have a warm cup of empathy. First round's on me.

This is not to say I was *better* than the English teacher. I didn't grade homework, classwork, or anything else on time and had stacks of ungraded paper by the end of the year. My lessons were more teacher-directed than I wanted, and I didn't set clear goals for much of anything. I just knew that underneath the raw and sometimes crass exteriors of my Harlem/Washington Heights–raised teens lay a need for someone to respond to their needs as people first, then as students. With the little means they had, they tried to make every person in that class feel special on their birthday and vouched for each other when one of them unjustly got into trouble.

By the end of May, the kids of 7H3 had pushed just about every other core teacher to the brink of retirement or off the deep end. But they had developed ways to advocate for themselves. As for their relationship with their English teacher, they learned quickly about petitioning, letter writing, and telling parents to call the school whenever they had collective issues. They did this, mind you, without my guidance. I'm not sure where they got the activist spirit,* but I certainly respected it. In retrospect, they were the first to teach me that homeroom classes often become a reflection of deeper truths about teachers, things we don't necessarily reveal openly to them about ourselves.

In the end what I found was this: When I took off my mask and invested myself in a group of kids, the homeroom became a home. For all of us.

---

* Grin.

WHITE NOISE
(ON BEHALF OF RUBEN REDMAN)

I still remember the day I found out. In the hallways, students surrounded Chucky, our legendary part-time floor assistant.

"You heard about the student who they shot?"

"Yeah, but I didn't know who it was."

"It was all over Univision. You remember, um, um, Redman
was the last name."

"RUBEN?"

"Yeah."

"Wow."

"Yeah."

I took a deep breath, incredulous until I got home. Then, I
watched the NY1 report online. Then it hit me. It was true.

> *A Bronx teen was killed in a triple shooting. It happened*
> *around 10 p.m. Monday at 1225 Gerard Avenue in*
> *Mount Eden.**

Stare into the eyes of a boy whose eyes glistened rather
than rolled

---

* This and other excerpts were used from the NY1 news report: "Teen Dies, Two
Wounded in Bronx Shooting," NY1 News, February 24, 2009, www.ny1.com
/content/news/94512/teen-dies—two-wounded-in-bronx-shooting.

Watch his skin deteriorate in a light powder
A finely tailored suit covering his shell of an exterior
This body used to contain dreams,
Jokes,
Laughs,
Emotions raw as the deal dealt to the young man . . .

Police say they believe two groups of men got into a fight over
some graffiti, resulting in Ruben Redman, 15, being shot
in the back of the head. He was taken to Lincoln Hospi-
tal where he was pronounced dead.

Imagine giving birth to a young man who will see the
    inside of a casket before you do
Imagine planting a seed into concrete and never seeing
    it sprout
Where once the ideas of a million men blossomed in his
    chromosomes
We replace those ideas with questions of potential and
    longing
Did we do enough? How do I play a role in this?

"There was some graffiti, a mark, that was made by one group
that was written over by the other group. They took this as
an insult," said Police Commissioner Ray Kelly. "The
group that was upset over the mark being written over ap-
proached one individual, took out a .45-caliber handgun,
and fired several shots."
Police have not yet made any arrests and are still investigat-
ing the incident.

Walking into a funeral home I've seen all too often
Young men and women walk side by side with their
    younger images

"Damn, remember how he used to be? Now, so grown."
The naive become adult, the short get closer to the
    heavens
The elder get grayer and the insolent gain wisdom
While mothers and daughters yell like fishing rods that
    never capture their catch
This observer's pupils dilate
Inspiration to proceed with his daily occupation . . .

The others were hospitalized with non-life-threatening wounds.

The news reporter replays repeatedly in my mind
Memories spiraling,
Enraged that people around me feel more apathy than
    rage
Another boy killed, another waste,
Another missed opportunity,
For you? Another good opportunity to tell people, "I
    told you so."
For me? Another opportunity to ignore you and say,
    "Never again.
Not my students."
My goal so much clearer than what I write on the
    board
Turning the knob to a frequency where
Everything else is white noise . . .

"I often wish that I could save everyone, but I'm a dreamer."
                    —Scarface, "Smile"

Ruben,
As one of my first students, I remember you as a portly one.
    Always dressed in funky colors, and had style for days when-
ever you weren't in uniform.

Never really in a gang, but had a tag name (think I didn't know about that, Trons?).

I'm almost certain, though, that you wouldn't have gotten into that other mess everyone else was into. You had dreams of doing really great things. Maybe a lawyer, doctor, or whatever other profession your parents encouraged from you. Both of them were there.

I remember my first year at your school, thinking how nervous but idealistic I was about the prospect of teaching my first batch of students. I remember cultivating that sense of urgency with all of you, that time was of the essence, and that what you're doing and what you see around you doesn't necessarily have to be yours. With that, I learned to push you hard, because I wanted to extract the best out of you.

We battled, and battled hard.

All in the name of seeing you reach your highest potential.

Even though I didn't get to teach you your eighth-grade year, I'd see you on my floor, on the block, with your friends, always with the nicest kicks, hanging out with girls.

Being young.

Graduating. With parents in tow. Parents I got really familiar with, as I called them about twice a month (once for you, once for your sister). So proud.

They say life's short, but no one ever defines what short is. You never expect that this would pertain to someone like you, Ruben. You weren't supposed to have this happen to you. You were supposed to mature out of this phase. You, more than anything, were caught up in the wrong place, wrong time.

And now you don't even get a chance to be at the right place. You're not getting that second chance. Hopefully you give your other friends a chance to see their lives as indispensable.

Ruben Redman, rest in peace. Stay good.

WHERE THE HUSTLE COMES FROM

"Eduardo, *levántate!*"

He wakes up with a splitting headache, growling stomach, eyes puffy and black from the lack of sleep and the active tossing and turning the night before. His mom gets home close to midnight from that job at the factory, an added stressor on his already fragile mind. He rushes out the door without breakfast and meets up with his boys on the corner, the only real family he feels he has.

He naps during first period and when he's awake, he can't concentrate because of the thoughts swirling in his mind. He thinks of his absent father, his mom, his younger brother, a cute girl he hasn't the nerve to ask on a date yet, a gang that keeps giving him a dirty eye. Then he thinks of the nice commercials he keeps seeing, of well-rounded families having breakfast. He thinks of everything except for what is being written on the chalkboard.

Suddenly he realizes the rest of the class is looking at him with chuckles and grins. He hears the teacher speaking to him.

". . . and why aren't you ever paying attention? This is why you're not doing very well and you never will."

Eduardo snaps.

"Ugh, leave me alone, miss."

"What do you mean, leave you alone? You're in my class and I gotta leave you alone now?"

"You and your speeches," he lets out with a sharp snicker.

Their back-and-forth continues until Eduardo finds a way to get a piece of quiet. "Can I go to the bathroom?"

"Just go," the teacher says, acknowledging that he may not come back.

He lounges in the hallway, temporarily relieved, savoring his freedom from that rigid box. The bell rings just in time for him to give back the pass; he runs out the door as the teacher shakes her head in disapproval in front of the rest of the class. After a lunch of Doritos and Tropical Fantasy, he's ready to act exactly how they've pegged him. He cracks jokes under his breath in the middle of exams. He might listen to the *one* teacher who pulls him out of class and starts to get to the bottom of his underlying issue, but, after school, he's the cool kid again. He's in command of his situation.

That is, until he comes home, and it's empty.

What do you say to him?

What do you say to kids whose only influences tell them to do as they say, not as they do? When they keep seeing their mom trying to recapture her youth but in the process neglecting her own children, who need her love so much? When she's going crazy in the main office when the situation didn't call for that and all the kids find out, so they're making fun of the crazy mom's kid? When their father shows up, pats their head, smacks their mom, tells her that she better come back, and, when she says no, runs out and throws a couple hundred dollars behind him?

When the only male role model they have works so hard that he comes home and lies on the sofa for hours on end? When there are days they don't even get to see him except in bed, resting for the next twelve-hour day? When the neighborhood gunrunner takes your students to the local parties and shows them how to interact with girls, and not in any way you'd approve of? When the girl who acts so innocent in class has already learned that the best way to interact with a man isn't through her intelligence or her strength, but with a wave of a finger and her lips? When your students are surrounded by failure and learn to accept it as the norm? When a school serves as the neighborhood training ground for prison?

When they are absent and you don't know why?

What is the definition of appropriate given everything you, as a teacher/educator/parent/counselor, have to do just to get your students in their seats, their graphite to the paper, and their minds locked into the material? Why are they absent? What are your standards?

When I look at a kid like Eduardo, I know how to approach him because I know the environment he's coming from. People are quick to blame individuals for their own circumstances, even though we can clearly trace the conditions of poverty to oppressive and racist policies already in place the moment the country was first founded.

Poor urban families are blamed for their own health issues, everything from diabetes to heart disease to asthma to obesity. But look at our closest food options. I used to think the food here was all right—until I visited the farmer's market in Union Square downtown and was astonished at all the fresh vegetables. Real lettuce, red tomatoes, and truly green broccoli. Natural apple juice and freshly picked oranges. Imagine if students in poverty uptown could come to school with such foods in their stomachs? But their parents more often settle for the unkempt vegetable aisle close to home or rely on the less expensive canned- and boxed-food aisles. Those same parents experienced Reaganomics, the crack infestation, police brutality, immigration reform, the growth of the prison-industrial complex, lead-tainted water, downgraded hospitals, and of course gentrification.

Considering the so-called "Third World" conditions right here in the United States of America, the concept of a First World is beyond me.

As teachers, we see the effects. When our students arrive at school malnourished and uncared for, they're treated like vagabonds. They act out, stealing from each other and screaming at their teachers. Teachers and administrators scrutinize them for every possible

disorder or dysfunction; while such kids can benefit from more substantial help than any individual can offer, many of them don't really
have a disorder at all. They just need someone to talk to them like
human beings. Yet, if they are not being misdiagnosed for some disability, they confront an instant bias against them in the classroom.
Some people who decide to teach for all the wrong reasons will
let their classism and racism creep through, stoking mistrust among
students toward an educational system they need.

We can't blame hip-hop for social inequity, war, infant mor-
tality rates, the rising cost of attending university, racism, or high
incarceration and unemployment rates. This is what our kids carry
in their backpacks every morning at least 180 days out of the year.

Our society still has the nerve to stand by the idea of personal
responsibility and accountability, shaming families for buying two-
hundred-dollar sneakers or rims for their cars instead of investing
in the stock market, as if projecting status is not one way to over-
come a real lack of power. The images we see of bling and pomp
usually represent a very small percentage of people truly living in
poverty, and that's what we don't really see. Many of the little gadgets
we see the kids with are secondhand, illegal devices, and if there are
liquor stores on every corner, it's partly because that's the one legal
potion people can use to get away from their daunting troubles.

The disconnect between the problem and the solution persists.
And it's not limited to my kids, either. Children all over the United
States and the world have their views on what education means to
them and how adults view the educational system in the country.
Where do we go from here?

When I argue about this with people, I hear, "But José, you made
it. You lived in the same environment these people did, and yet look
at you now. You're successful and have a promising future." Usually,
such a person comes from a household where the parents were successful and a family that's been similarly successful for generations. It
never comes from someone who's been through similar straits.

I am one of the fortunate ones. I had a mother who, for all

her flaws, pushed me in the right direction; a good set of schools, both private and public; and enough people who believed in me—along with a dose of stubbornness, an aptitude for academics, and a chip on my shoulder that only grew the more people disregarded my abilities. Had any of these factors fallen out of place, I wouldn't have been as successful. I know people who walked a similar path as I did, had parents and a culture around them that emphasized education, and even went to better schools than I did—and who didn't do as well economically. And I'm a teacher.

It always goes back to the same root: our educational system is meant to keep certain people docile and uneducated. These simple changes we ask for, like character development, extra accommodations for students who struggle with state tests, and a more supportive school system as a whole for all parties involved, are always regarded as "too expensive" or "pending" some litigation that usually gets drowned out by some other mess. Some of these simple adjustments may have worked in individual schools, but as a system, we're just not doing well.

So what can we do? Maybe that's the better question. After a recent conversation with a younger teacher, I thought I'd list some things that might be helpful with the socio-emotional part of this education process. I'm learning along the way, so suggestions and comments are welcome. Note that some of these will make you say "duh," but I find that too many people who work with children (and adults) don't incorporate this at all.

1. **Get that respect:** First build the foundation for what you're going to do with them, then you can take it however you like. Some teachers are more comfortable with regimentation and others are a bit looser. However you choose to go, you have to build the respect first.

2. **Don't try to change them, try to know them:** We're still too inundated with images of the teacher who outright changes a student overnight. It's just not true. Try just getting to know them and maybe there'll

be an exchange of learned experiences. Change here
becomes implicit.

3. **Show up to things sporadically**: Anytime I
   show up for a talent show, a basketball game, or just
   passing by another of their classes, I earn points in
   my respect count.

4. **Talk to them**: Obviously, if you're not talking to them
   personally, one-on-one, then you're not going to earn that
   respect. Even if that inappropriately behaved student acts
   out in class after you've had a conversation, you'll see
   through that and not stress yourself out too much.

5. **Humble yourself**: Working with students whose
   background may be different than yours is the primary
   job. Forget the benefits, the health care, the days off, and
   the discounts. Like actors, we play roles in students' lives,
   and the number-one thing to know is that, no matter
   how great a job you're doing, there's still the next day.
   And the next. And the next.

6. **Celebrate and accentuate the positive**: At
   some point along the way that year, I forgot how good
   I have it, relatively speaking. A grand majority (I'd say
   three-quarters) of my students actually try their best
   and have great potential to do well, despite themselves.
   I don't have all honor students, but I've found good
   returns on my investments in them. Yet I let the negative
   cloud my judgment about entire classes, and that was a
   problem. So not only did I get back on my feet (with a
   little help from my friends), I organized an awards show
   for the floor, and it worked two ways: it celebrated the
   achievements of those who try and those who excel,
   while allowing all the teachers on the floor to share in
   the pride of teaching. It's really those little things that
   make a difference. Seriously.

As I review these tips, I think of the children and adults who have
never felt loved, who feel so hopeless that they preferred to stay in
prison so they'll stay out of trouble, who die for the most trivial

things, who give favors of all varieties just so they can continue living their lives, however miserable. Imagine if just that pat on the back or that good talking-to might have tilted their sails in the right direction.

But in the grand scheme of things, I'm only one educator. Even one who has a platform that's widely distributed can't revolutionize the whole educational system. I myself still have a long way to go. And there are certain things I cannot leave behind. I still struggle with the same health issues as many of those from my neighborhood. I can't count how many times I've had taxis race past me, gotten bad service at a restaurant because they thought I wouldn't tip well, or been given the least professional doctor.

And, like Eduardo, the world seemed much vaster than I could handle because the world around me was tough enough as it stood. Yet these murky experiences give our souls texture. They push us to hustle for every opportunity for a better life than the one we were originally handed.

As for the Eduardos: an astute teacher would be wise to hold firm, suppress all these emotions, and ask what's wrong. The student might not be able to tell you, but you may be the only rest stop they get in this journey.

P.S. If at any point, you feel like you've failed—and you've absolutely tried your best—learn to say to yourself, "It's going to get better."

THE WORLD IS YOURS,
THE WORLD IS YOURS

You should have seen my face the first time I tried to log into my website using a NYC DOE computer and it said "Blocked."

At first I didn't get it. Just a few days before, I hadn't had any issue getting onto my website to check and respond to comments, but something about seeing the filter screen made me smirk knowingly.

When I started blogging in 2003, I used a pseudonym (which I'm not revealing here). I wanted a mask of invisibility while I got myself together and honed my voice. I blogged from my unemployed phase to well into my teaching career, by which point my posts were receiving hundreds of comments and regular recognition from the creators of the now-defunct blogging site Xanga. The more I got to know other bloggers across the country, the more I sought to make those connections less anonymous. Meeting up with them and seeing whether they matched their alter egos gave me an uncanny sense of purpose, as if we all blogged anonymously to shield ourselves from judgment and real-world repercussions.

Back then, I wrote about everything under the sun. I went from radical anti-Dubya posts to lists of regular readers who deserved awards for the most random reasons. Most of the posts ranted about the state of our country, highlighting the intersections of race and class and how they affected our neighborhoods. Other times, I delved into life in the 'hood and how it felt as a college grad to come back to a place often bereft of positive role models. I got to have fun every so often with posts, too, but without an editor or a muse my writing had no real filter. When I started teaching, I saw my writing about teaching as an extension of the radical essays I had typed over the previous year.

Over a three-year span, I would meet more than 150 regular readers through my site, hailing from Boston to San Francisco and a dozen places in between, a few of whom were teachers. Almost all of them felt like friends I never met face to face; once we did meet, our conversations often flowed naturally from our midnight exchanges online. To this day, I call some of these people my closest friends.

In 2006, my friend Harmony Thompson, whom I met on Xanga, nudged me to get my own domain name and create a "brand" for myself. Another online friend and fantastic writer, Amber Cabral, told me how she had transitioned from an anonymous site to a full-blown self-hosted site. It didn't cost too much, and most of the fancy tricks I had at my disposal on Xanga were much easier to do on WordPress, especially if I did everything under my real name. I went from generalist to specialist, trying to explain to my readers my transition from rebel raconteur to urban educator, and how all the things I felt passionate about played out when I started to teach. If I set aside a few dollars to get it hosted, I would have creative control. I just had to figure out a name.

I typed into Google: "José Vilson."

I found a bunch of Brazilians who used "Vilson" as a middle name and a few minor-league soccer sites. My pseudonym came up a couple of times, but I stubbornly thought I could do better than that. I didn't care how many losers in Rio de Janeiro shared parts of my name. I wanted to be number one on the Interwebs.

Oops, I'm sorry, I lied. I wanted number one, two, three, four, and five.*

As I considered whether to make the leap from anonymity to a new blog under my name, a number of questions paddled in my stream:

---

* Sampled from KRS-One's "Step Into A World."

- Why leave the safe confines of a blog where I had already amassed what felt like thousands of comments (more than a hundred on my "Fuck Bush" post alone)?
- How could I leave more than three hundred subscribers after almost five years?
- Would I still be able to start some shit at will through my writing with no consequences?

I leapt anyway.

The José Vilson (www.thejosevilson.com) was born, both online and in spirit. I tried to do some of the cool things my other friends had done with their blogs, but even with my computer science degree, I felt way in over my head. Before I even knew how to blog, I wrote entries by saving a text file and uploading it to a special page on my site. It felt so clunky that I wondered whether it was worth it. After I fully learned WordPress, I experimented with magazine-style writing, thinking my audience might gravitate to what they saw in more mainstream publications like *TIME* or *Newsweek*. My voice felt more distant, more subject-oriented, less personal. I thought elevating my voice meant trying to write like a journalist would.

Without Xanga providing a consistent stream of blogs to read, I had no choice but to go by recommendations, nearly all of whom were mainstream media writers. But none of those writers were doing what I was doing, so I couldn't emulate their voices well. I needed my own. If I kept writing like them, I couldn't write like *me*.

After a few months, I settled on writing mostly about teaching, because at least I knew *what* and *how* I would write. I decided that I would be the first Black-Latino NYC/Lower East Side educator/poet/blogger—and I wouldn't compromise my message for fear of retribution from the school district, board, administration, or any other person who even remotely knew me.

Of course, I had to steal a bit from the people I wanted to emulate. The first blog I had ever read that dealt specifically with New York City schools was *NYC Educator*.* Dubbed the "Daily Show"

---

* www.nyceducator.com.

of education blogging, *NYC Educator* intertwined local education politics with stories from the classroom, using a sharp yet unassuming sense of humor. Discovering his writing felt refreshing at a time when most education writing felt so polite and lacking in passion. He pulled no punches and, after we developed a friendship, served as a mentor both in blogging and teaching. His blog, along with *Norm's Notes, JD2718*, and the *Pissed Off Teacher*,* all of whom were classroom bloggers writing dangerously, represented what I considered the best in NYC education blogging at the time, and I wanted to sit at the cool table with them.

Miss Profe, another education blogger, introduced me to other underrepresented bloggers like *The Field Negro*, whose blog is so notorious now, I have to scroll past fifty fans and fifty trolls just to comment.† I started to see the collection of blogs I read as a collage of different influences to the voice I wanted to achieve, from those written by Latino activists, like *The Unapologetic Mexican*, to progressive math teachers like Dan Meyer (*dy/dan*).‡ Every blog I perused left an impression, shaping and pushing me to a more credible version of my blogging voice.

I got the same feeling I did back in college when finding my social interest clubs, especially since I was usually the only person of color in any given group. These virtual spaces gave me a sense of community and solidarity with communities that were otherwise not available to me in the so-called real world. These safe spaces allowed for my frustrations as a teacher, as an activist, as a person of color, as well as allowing me to see myself in both a historical and a contemporary context. In those spaces, my experiences held precedence with others before me, and would continue to hold precedence with people after me. I soon came to find out that the space I was creating with *The José Vilson* would combine

---

* normsnotes2.blogspot.com; jd2718.org; pissedoffteacher.blogspot.com.
† field-negro.blogspot.com.
‡ theunapologeticmexican.org; blog.mrmeyer.com.

all those elements in a way no one else had. I still felt like a part of a whole.

Dropping my pseudonym and blogging under my real name, inevitably, got me in trouble. A few teachers and administrators at my school caught wind of my writing and told my principal, "José Vilson blogs, you know." This was not shared with a sense of pride, but rather with a bit of bitterness and aversion, as if my blogging would attract undue negative attention to our school or spur gossip (something these same people constantly shared behind their doors).

Gossip about bloggers includes, but is not exclusive to:

"Is this post about me? Oh, look, it might be, I'm not sure."

"He got an award for this and a ton of readers. How many people did he have to pay off?"

"Which kid is he talking about here?"

"Is he doing this blogging on school time? Shouldn't he be focused on kids?"

"This important person reads his blog, but I didn't think to read it for anything other than indirect jabs at me. Let me go look."

Education bloggers generally don't wish harm on their kids or their administration. They just want to do the best job possible, air their frustrations, and reflect on becoming better practitioners. Insinuations from those wishing to snitch on their colleagues for their own betterment only hurt trust and undermine bloggers' ability to communicate to the rest of the world effectively.

Fed up with the bull, I asked for a closed-door meeting with my principal. Without getting into too much into detail, we had a heart-to-heart in which I laid out my intention to remain a member of the school community and reiterated that I believed in his vision. I told him that nothing I wrote in my posts would affect my professionalism in the classroom. (I wanted to get a joke in about how I'd have to write all this up in a book someday, but I totally missed my chance.) He responded positively. Overall, I walked out of that meeting empowered, but I know that not many education bloggers feel the same way when they walk out of closed-door meetings with their administrators, especially in so-called "right to work" states.

After hashing it out with a few friends and reflecting on the worst-case scenarios, I came up with a few rules for my blog:

1. Never talk about my principal.
2. Never mention my colleagues unless they are in the process of retiring at the moment of my writing.
3. Never use students' names unless they explicitly give me permission.

Education blogger and writer Bud Hunt once said that transparency isn't always about how much we share overall, but how much we will share *of* what we share. Maybe I can't tell you everything that goes on in my teaching, but what I do share I can expound on in great detail, enough so you can take a stroll in my size thirteens. I couldn't proclaim realness if I didn't talk about my job as a concrete set of events that actually happened, but I risked losing the trust and respect of others.

These are the breaks.

Having concrete rules also gave me the freedom to do other things in my writing, like curse. I used only the most non-gendered words,* and deployed them indiscriminately against people and ideas I felt deserved a sharp dose of vitriol. Cursing isn't just a way to vent. It serves a purpose: to shock the usually puritan education audiences and aggressively advance ideas about the need for change.

I don't doubt that some of my linguistic shenanigans activated the NYC DOE's Internet filters. Yet I also kept hearing that the DOE had bookmarked my site. When *Gotham Schools*—now *Chalkbeat NY*—became NYC's go-to education news site, people frequently arrived at my site based on its recommendations.† Yet my blog still couldn't bypass the filter.

---

* Except "motherfucker." I used that word twice. I also used the word "motherfucking" seven times, but mostly for parody. As if there should be any other use.
† chalkbeat.org.

My site was popular in the NYC district, but only within the central offices. It was blocked from the rest of the intranet, including the 1,700 schools under its umbrella. People used computers with administrative access to bypass the filter. Somehow, the rest of the country was more progressive than my own city.

My opinions on education had to get out somehow. Every school year, I found myself inundated with words in mandatory meetings that were seldom meaningful. I noticed that my preparatory and professional periods gave me no time to reflect on my preparation or my profession. After graduating from City College in 2007, which marked the end of my time in the Teaching Fellows program, I didn't have the same support group with which to air my grievances or the same mentors to help me along. With a twelve-hour schedule, including transportation time and paper grading, I had little time for social activism on a meaningful scale. But I spent an hour or so every Sunday, Monday, Tuesday, and Thursday writing long blog posts. I wanted to advocate, to influence, to push the bar further.

As my blog grew from rinky-dink teacher diary to teacher-essayist hub, I noticed the growing influence of the wider Internet, the proliferation of social media, and their potential for interrupting the usual okeydoke bloggers often engaged in (usually while catapulting their Twitter followers into the 60K range with cosmetic, cursory content). Education technology evangelists, many of whom called themselves teachers, settled on talking about tech tools and reciprocal back-patting, or what some might term "hugging it out." They seemed immune to events that challenged their insulated ideas. They mainly wrote things that would elicit comments reading "Right on!" and "You're the greatest!" They'd discuss breaking down the silos in silos, peeking out the window of the silo only to walk back in where the rest of their friends were.

Over time, I went from narrow radical to macro-radical.

By the same token, clinging to a narrative of "everything outside of our vision is evil" didn't make sense to me either. In social media and beyond, the education conversation cried out for nuance. I begged for solid arguments, for understanding people's true intent, and for looking at these conversations as a set of systems. Railing against one set of reforms means nothing if we don't advocate for another set of reforms that work. Educators *have* to get involved in planning curriculum and pedagogy. We also have to believe in ourselves as powerful change agents or else we perpetuate the same power structures we say we're against.

By participating in these conversations through my writing, I made connections in interesting ways. A reader and now friend, Dr. John Holland, introduced me to two men, John Norton, editor and moderator of the Teacher Leaders Network, and Dr. Barnett Berry, president of the Center for Teaching Quality. CTQ, an action group/think tank out of Carrboro, North Carolina, asked me to contribute a chapter to a book project called *Teaching 2030*—my first co-author tag. The book's thesis centered on how we can change schools and the teaching profession meaningfully to meet the needs of our students now and in the future.

Through my contribution to *Teaching 2030*, I came upon the work of educator (and writer hero) Renee Moore, whose blog pushed me to consider how to discuss actual classroom experience as I continued to hone my "teacher policy" voice. I connected with Iowa educator Shannon C'de Baca, New York English educator Ariel Sacks, author of *Whole Novels for the Whole Class: A Student-Centered Approach*, and Florida educator and Apple professional developer Emily Vickery, and dozens of teachers under the CTQ umbrella who knew how to ask questions with a little humor, grace, and gumption that prompted authorities to reconsider their positions. Our long discussions, both virtual and face-to-face and usually prompted by John Norton, hammered home the idea of having one foot in the classroom and the other foot firmly in the rest of the world. Code-switching so everyone hears you was the objective. It reminded me of when activists back in the day used to say, "Don't give anyone an excuse to ignore you."

CTQ's mission was to frame our message so that it could reach fellow teachers, supervisors, parents, and policy makers alike, while also capturing our broader intentions for better schools. How could we focus less on airing grievances and more on developing solutions and working with people who have completely different worldviews and insights?

Playing well with others in this virtual adult sandbox turned out to work well in unexpected ways. When education professor Michael Petrilli of the Fordham Institute compiled lists of top Twitter feeds for education policy in 2012 and 2013, I contended both times that using Klout scores (his method) to measure education policy replicated biases about who belongs on such lists.

Normally, I don't pay much mind to lists, awards, or recognition insofar as I keep doing my own thing. But I would be remiss if I didn't knock on his door to remind him that people of color exist. After a short debate on Twitter, Petrilli revised his list—which originally only had only one person of color (Michelle Rhee), along with just seven women, and no active teachers whatsoever—to include friend and former educator Sabrina Stevens . . . and me, the only active teacher on the list.* I appreciated the accolade, but only because it meant I also got to advocate for more people, more women, and more educators who dedicate themselves to speaking about education policy in a powerful way.

The invisible man just became visible.

If you believe there are just two sides to education reform (I don't), then it's obvious which side looks more diverse than the other at first glance. Michelle Rhee, John Legend, Geoffrey Canada, and a host of others readily stand out alongside Joel Klein, Eli Broad, and Bill Gates. They may disagree on some issues, but are all part of a corporate-focused, pseudo-technocratic version of education reform. We need visible people of color in the pro-whole-

---

* I would be remiss if I didn't mention that friend and education writer Audrey Watters and the Teach for America account also made the list. So it goes.

child movement. (Doesn't "pro-whole-child" sound a whole lot better than "anti-testing"?) The elevation of Chicago Teachers Union president Karen Lewis, as well as the likes of education professors Linda Darling-Hammond, Pedro Noguera, and Lisa Delpit, have changed the dynamic some, but we still have a ways to go. The lists and awards matter less than the idea of inclusion.

By engaging with the likes of Petrilli on Twitter, *The José Vilson* became a more established entity, one that could confront ideas on an independent platform with an educator's voice. Until more educators of color step up to the mantle, we'll continue to see ourselves denied within the margins of list-makers' existences. My blogging went from serving my own interests and reflecting on my thoughts to influencing others—and encouraging people to say what they think out loud, with little compromise. The education blogging world needs someone who can ask the hard questions about inequity, race, and class. Perhaps that person can work outside of the pseudo-dichotomy.

Give me some room, please.

YES, I STILL WANT TO TEACH

I swear to God they can't make me quit this shit.

I promised myself I wouldn't quit so readily. If, for some reason, I lost the passion that wakes me up at 5:30 in the morning and drags me almost an hour in transit to my job, I could be convinced then. Even when people want me to leave, even when the gossip comes raining down, even when our state and federal governments continue to deprofessionalize our jobs and cut our funding, I'm stubborn enough to say I can't stop.

I get that I've made myself a target. I attract a certain kind of attention at my school for my political leanings. I can't wear all-black on Malcolm X's birthday or the first day of Black History Month and not get a little side-eye. I can't lock the door in my homeroom and write "nigger" on the board without catching a little heat. Doing these things in our age of so-called colorblindness has its drawbacks.

But I was born to do this.

I have always seen teaching as more than a job. While people list numerous reasons to teach in public schools—job security through unions, stable paychecks, educator discounts for name-brand products like Apple and the *New York Times*, family-friendly work hours—those have always felt like thick, tasty icing on the cake of playing a small part in changing students' lives. I wanted to be a change agent, and I decided that the best way I could do that would be teaching the primary make-or-break subject in K–12: math.

I don't mean to suggest that all teachers must have an innate pull toward the profession and that those who don't should not get a teaching license. But when I step into a classroom, it feels like everything else I have done with my life until now was meant to direct me there, like everything I went through was training for this.

It's a feeling that brings me back to Dr. Martin Luther King Jr. Ever since I learned more about him in college, the term "reluctant leader" has always stood out for me. As with plenty of us who regularly speak up about injustices, he seemed like he could have stayed home and chilled with the homies. But once he had a platform, he knew he had to speak—and he knew how to do so in ways that his listeners would understand. He swayed masses toward the optimism that permeated the civil rights movement. Dr. King was not the first person to lead reluctantly. His is just the story that spoke to me.

Here's the story that puts me at risk of getting fired. Without it I wouldn't have a blog or even a career. It happened my second year of teaching. My eighth-graders were learning how to translate verbal expressions into mathematical equations when I heard a booming voice in the hallway. I didn't know what it was, but I knew it didn't bode well for someone. One of my students, who had gone to the bathroom, came back and whispered to me in the middle of my lesson, "Mr. Vilson, they're talking about you. It's your bulletin board." I deflected her concern and got back to work on one of my favorite math topics.

But after dismissing the class, I imagined the discussion outside my door:

"This is a bulletin board?"

"Look at these shitty pieces of work!"

"This isn't very organized!"

"How does this guy even get away with this?"

I shrugged it off, maintaining my composure until lunch, when I developed a knot in my stomach. It was true that I'd thrown a few pieces of student work up on my bulletin board without any real consideration for whether they were in perfect rows or accented with multicolored construction paper. If the purpose of a bulletin board was to display work in a way that makes students feel proud, mine didn't communicate how much I loved their work. Other teachers' bulletin boards featured rainbow highlights and bubble lettering. They often printed rubrics from online generators like Rubistar that showed the dimensions that determine students' grades: "This paper shows poor thinking skills" would get one point, while "This work demonstrates clear mathematical knowledge" would get four. The assumption was that kids would glean from this a path to improving whatever skills the rubric was judging.

I didn't like boxes all that much.

Later in the day, my assistant principal came to my classroom to admonish me. She criticized my bulletin board, along with my general classroom aesthetics. In fact, the administrator told me that, due to my classroom, I would receive an unsatisfactory rating—a huge smack in the face given how much gusto I brought to my job.

The teacher evaluation system at that time worked in binary: either we were Satisfactory (S) or Unsatisfactory (U). The incentive for getting S ratings throughout the first three years was tenure, or what should be dubbed "due process." Due process is a way of making sure that teachers can't get fired unjustifiably. On the other hand, according to my union rep, getting even one U could keep new teachers in probationary limbo for as long as the administrator in charge sees fit. The cynics in the teachers' lounge would say, "The admins will give you a U for anything! Even for a crummy bulletin board!"

Rumors followed:

"Are they trying to get rid of Vilson?"

"Is he not as good as they say he is?"

"Was he just protected last year because he was cool with the old assistant principal?"

Others seemed to relish the situation, for reasons that weren't clear to me. Honestly, I didn't know what I'd done. I didn't feel paranoid, but when I didn't have the kids in front of me, I felt my head spinning. The rationale seemed to be that the unopened boxes in my classroom and my crooked bulletin board meant that my students weren't learning. I spent my prep periods looking around the room, trying to understand why any of this mattered to my career or me, but I tried to figure out why anyone would want me to feel like I couldn't trust anyone, much less the people who were supposed to lead me. I always felt prepared, the students were generally engaged, and I never felt afraid to experiment with my lessons.

Looking back on it now, it felt inane, and it could have been avoided entirely had there been a clear set of expectations. Instead, my administrators spent entire professional development periods parading us through the school to demonstrate excellent bulletin boards. Those of us who didn't have the eye for aesthetics were confused, but because of the severe implications of receiving a U before getting due process rights, it made me feel like I was working less against any one person than against an entire system of people whose sole purpose was to nitpick in the name of accountability.

If it makes no sense to you, it made even less sense to me, a second-year teacher with little experience with the punitive culture of the NYC Department of Education. My graduate program never taught me about the importance of seat alignments or multicolored charts as a means to get my students engaged in the actual material. I just threw a few things together so I could focus on my lesson planning. A new teacher like me needed professional development, not intimidation and humiliation in front of students who happened to be in the hallway. The disproportionate response to something as minor as a bulletin board might have made me laugh if not for my tenuous relationship (at best) with the administration at that point. Now there was a "legitimate" basis for destroying the life of an untenured teacher from whom the children actually enjoyed learning.

Under immense pressure and with no real support from my administration, I turned back to MLK. I listened to his "I've Been to the Mountaintop" speech while I reflected on my predicament:

Well, I don't know what will happen now. We've got some difficult days ahead. But it really doesn't matter with me now, because I've been to the mountaintop. And I don't mind. Like
anybody, I would like to live a long life. Longevity has its place.
But I'm not concerned about that now. I just want to do God's
will. And He's allowed me to go up to the mountain. And I've
looked over. And I've seen the Promised Land. I may not get
there with you. But I want you to know tonight, that we, as a
people, will get to the promised land!*

The tears streamed down my face as I replayed the speech on
YouTube. Let me be clear: I didn't equate the threats against my
burgeoning career with the death threats faced by Dr. King. But
my fear of being disconnected from my passion and my people
reaffirmed that I couldn't sit passively while my higher-ups tried
to strip me of my position arbitrarily. I had to live fearlessly. My
vision for my students should last far beyond my own existence as
their teacher.

I decided to take action. My math coach consulted with me,
my fellow teachers pleaded with me, and my blog commenters em-
pathized with me. "You'll soon learn that you've got to pick and
choose your battles," my math colleagues said. "Some stuff you can
disagree with them and say 'Fuck 'em,' and other stuff you just gotta
do if you want to stay here." But none of it helped as much as Dr.
King did. So I did the best thing I could think of: I posted the
"mountaintop" quote on my desk, front and center.

"Mr. Vilson, what does that mean?" my students asked. I
wanted to say that I felt like I needed MLK's words now more than
ever, that I still wanted to teach, that even if I didn't make it to the
end of the year because I kept hearing threats of a U in my ear, I'd

---

* Dr. Martin Luther King Jr., speech delivered April 3, 1968, the night before
his assassination, at Mason Temple in Memphis, Tennessee. The full audio
and a transcript are available at www.americanrhetoric.com/speeches
/mlkivebeentothemountaintop.htm.

be satisfied knowing that I had tried my best to get my students ready for high school, the next step toward college. But I stammered and told them they would understand one day.

My lesson plans became more passionate, more urgent. I had never cared so much in my life about any job I ever had now that I was certain my days were numbered. Meanwhile, the same assistant principal who'd given me a hard time about my bulletin board continued to try to intimidate me, showing me fake standards from an obscure document she'd found online that contained a line about classroom aesthetics. I remember trembling with anger when she first came into my classroom, but by the end of my meeting, the anger had turned to fear; those stomach knots came back. The minute she stepped out of the door, I yelled a good "FUCK!," flipped over every desk in the room, and ripped off my tie.

In my head, of course. I had a class next period.

This is something teachers deal with far too frequently. My corporate jobs were so different. In that environment, when you get pissed off at a coworker, you can retreat to a cubicle or the bathroom and isolate yourself. You can find your inner smoker and go outside, even if just to inhale someone's secondhand smoke to alleviate the anger. Most people in the corporate world don't need to be told to leave their emotional baggage at work; they just do.

Teachers have to wait for their assigned time to use the restroom, eat lunch, to go from being Ms. or Mr. So-and-So to having a first name. Teachers can't blow off steam until their schedules say Prep or Lunch. In the meantime, they are surrounded by younger people who have enough problems of their own and expect the adults around them to get it together. Kids in middle school aren't in tune with most other people's feelings because they're still learning about their own. They get a pass for not noticing. Every so often, though, one of them does notice and asks what's wrong. As teachers, it catches us off guard and we have to say, "Nothing. It's all good."

Adults, on the other hand, often exacerbate issues between other adults. The more support teachers need, the more administrators seem willing to come in and tell them what they're doing wrong. They brag to their fellow administrators about how many U ratings they can give out. They write about their teachers in on-line discussion boards while pretending they know nothing about the Internet. They seem to hope that enough cracks in the teachers' shells will split apart their existence.

In my second year I started to develop a derisive view of ad-ministrators from the local level on up. I came to see assistant prin-cipals as nothing more than people who didn't want to teach, but wanted a job in education by any means. Before New York State revamped its accreditation system, when there were administration shortages, school leaders only needed eighteen credits from their districts to get licensed. Going from a system where administrators need *some* classroom experience to one where they don't even need to see a classroom hurts everyone involved.

I started to see everyone above principals as paper pushers and the sycophants who pretended to love them. A superintendent would walk into a building accompanied by a sea of ties and blouses, messaging away on their BlackBerrys, ready to tell teach-ers what to do without ever having met them. They'd preach the word of their favorite education guru or the latest directive from the chancellor and hold it over teachers that they didn't get to read the secret e-mails sent at four in the morning. They were power players, not instructional leaders.

Everyone had to kiss the right butt, speak the right lingo, cite the right people, and follow the right protocols. Everyone had to innovate within the confines of what their immediate supervisor said, or they'd get subjected to questions and more questions, a method of intimidation when giving a U rating wasn't enough. Everyone had to keep a record of everything said in a meeting, even if it amounted to nothing. Everyone needed to obey, obey, obey.

Or else.

Especially in a subject like math, where experts were few and far between, administrators would find a way to step around your content expertise, find a flaw, and try to exploit it. If you didn't say "Yes" to everything and everyone, if you didn't smile or say "Good morning" when they wanted, if you didn't jump at the chance to work with them, if you didn't constantly ask them for favors or advice, if you weren't helpful in the ways they asked you to be helpful, if you didn't smile or shuck and jive at their will, then you were the problem. You were a threat because you didn't go along with the program. It wasn't my nature to make people feel warm and fuzzy about themselves; I spent enough energy just trying to get kids to learn math. Some administrators who see themselves as weak in one area overcompensate by waving their power around in the hopes that newer folks won't notice. But I didn't have tenure yet, so I had to keep my mouth shut.

Not every administrator is knowledgeable, and perhaps that was the greatest flaw in my assumptions during my second year.

I write this knowing I've survived and thrived as a teacher. My resolve wouldn't allow me to get off this ride. For the first time in my life, I felt like I could do this for the better part of forever. Yes, I've had things stolen. Yes, I've gotten upset, furious, enraged in front of my students. Yes, I still have to work within the dimensions given to me. Yes, I've learned to work with other adults I don't agree with. Yes, some of my kids didn't do well academically.

Yes, I still want to teach.

SAFER SPACES

"That's so gay."
"What a fuckin' homo!"
"No, no, that's it. You're gay and that's it."
"¡Que maldito maricón del diablo!" *(What a damn faggot from hell!)*

These are the kinds of quotes one hears when working in socially conservative neighborhoods, where the largely immigrant parents carry intolerance handed down by their own parents and by neighbors who grew up hating LGBT people. The type of homophobia that is common in mostly white communities, even so-called progressive communities, can also happen in places where people assume there's unity in the face of oppression. These phobias only exacerbate the pressures of puberty, making kids who are already unsure about themselves fear that other people's sexuality might have negative repercussions for them. Ridiculous.

Observing kids regularly, though, I have noticed that the idea of fluid sexuality has come to the fore. The rainbow paraphernalia my kids wear and the songs they listen to have definitely caught my eye and encouraged the kind of classroom I want to cultivate, one based on an understanding of their interests and lives as people, not just students with test scores attached. As an LGBT ally, I have also had to look beyond the concept of "tolerance," which speaks less to our children's humanity than does full acceptance.

Recently two of my former students came to visit me for my birthday and greeted me with hugs. It was cute, really. I was excited to know that they still cared enough about me to visit. Now, the taller of the two, whom I'll call J, said, "So guess what, Mr. V?" Normally, I expect to hear something like "chicken butt"—typical kiddie business. Instead he said:

"Me and some of your other former students are bi. And JD, well, he's actually bi, too. You remember that time when he came up to you last year and said, 'I got something to tell you,' and he said that I was gay? Well it's that he really wanted to say that he was bi, but he didn't know how you would react so he didn't say anything."

I blinked hard. Twice.

I replied coyly, "Well, I knew all of that, and I'm happy that you all have enough trust in me that you almost revealed yourselves to me. That takes courage. And when you see him, tell him he can talk to me anytime."

We said our goodbyes and I turned on my iPod and hopped into the train station, reflecting on this new information. Looking back, I couldn't imagine all the harassment JD had faced when he made that announcement to his friends. I wished that he had approached me then, because of the father-son relationship I believe we fostered over the two years I taught him. But I also realized it was selfish to want him to have told me something like that when, in hindsight, he was still searching for the answers himself.

How do we as educators recognize each person's humanity? How do we change the culture within classrooms where, too often, students who don't know any better speak coarsely about others—primarily out of their own insecurity? Middle school is challenging enough for our students. By allowing words like "faggot," "*maricón*," and, for that matter, "nigger," "spic," "chink," "bitch," or "slut," we become complicit in adding to their challenges. I rarely got any indication of my students' personal (sexual) lives or how their secrets affected their behavior in the classroom.

I hoped that the next time JD saw me, he would have gotten

my message that his sexuality is not a flaw, but an essential part of him.

Since I first formulated my thoughts on sexuality and being an LGBT ally in a blog post entitled "Goodbye Yellow Brick Road," society has shifted a bit toward full acceptance. In 2012 my home state of New York became the largest state to propose and ratify full marriage for all couples. Major corporations like the NBA, Major League Baseball, and Google have run commercials in support of LGBT youth. While cynics see an underlying profit motive that gives such businesses an incentive to align themselves with gay rights and marriage equality, I also genuinely think people are sincere in their motives for promoting LGBT marriage as more people reveal their stories.

When I first presented this very story to my readers in January 2008, I got a wave of responses from fellow educators. At this point, my blog went from a journal to an open forum to touch on controversial issues. Few—if any—blogs wanted to delve into this topic, as discussions about societal ills didn't get many views or comments. Yet, this one moved the needle a bit.

The first comment came from Damian Bariexca, New Jersey educator, social-media maven, and overall good guy:

> This is my 8th year co-teaching a Multicultural Studies class at my high school, and my students spend 2-3 weeks studying, researching, & discussing GLBT history & contemporary issues. It never ceases to amaze me how many kids feel that "fag" or the pejorative use of "gay" is completely mainstream & acceptable; I'm even finding this among gay youth. What's more, even the most progressive of the bunch will usually deny to their dying breath any analogy between "fag" and "dyke" and the racial epithets you mentioned above. Part of me hopes that's just them thinking too concrete and literally, but another part of me despairs for their logic.

The third from Luz (yes):

> It is very hard for our students to sometimes share their thoughts, questions, experiences, and sexuality with adults. There

is a fear of judgment, rejection, labeling, lack of compassion and understanding.

Taylor, former New Orleans educator, responded with this:

> I once had a gay student tell me that he was bullied daily in his science class and that when he told the teacher she told him that he was bringing it on himself by his dress and behavior. I wanted to go to admin with this, and he didn't want to let me. He did agree to let me do that, and when I did I don't think anything was done. If the AP's reaction/facial expression is any indication, I'm afraid he may have received more of the same. It makes me mad. Next time I think I'll just listen and be sympathetic unless I'm sure admin will take it seriously. (like, in a different school.)
>
> I have a picture of this student up on my file cabinet next to my desk, and many other students comment on it w/ a snarky attitude. That's the Bible belt for ya.

Months later, this anonymous comment came in:

> I agree with everything above; I am a gay high school student, in the bible belt, and have not yet come out to even friends and family. I am not so much afraid that they will abandon me, but I am afraid that they will never be able to think of me in the same way. I really appreciate you doing this for these teens.

I didn't think I had done anything special, and didn't know what would happen to this young man. But the next time I saw JD, in the spring of 2012, he was a few inches taller, with the same crisp smile he liked to show off. When I gave him a half-handshake, half-hug, I noticed he had a diamond ring on his left hand. Before he even pointed across the street at his better half, I told him how proud I was of him as a person and how glad I was that he had the opportunity to get married in New York State.

SNITCHES OPEN STITCHES

"Snitches get stitches": it's an oft-repeated axiom in urban communities, dictating that anyone willing to share incriminating information with law enforcement should receive physical punishment for their actions. The idea has in recent years been broadened to include any authority figure—including teachers. This enrages me; snitches used to be strictly defined as people who divulged information in order to alleviate their own punishment by law enforcement. That mentality left bodies strewn and candles lit all over my old 'hood—and decreased our potential to empower each other in the face of police who didn't understand us.

In the classroom, "snitches" are often the teachers themselves, reporting erratic behaviors and trends to the principal and guidance counselors. Many times, teachers don't forewarn students about the behavior they're about to report. Some teachers might ask "Is everything all right?" and get a nod for a response. But over time, even the most patient among us have to report problem behaviors to the appropriate authority. Usually it leads to preventative services that work for children, like offering counseling sessions or monthly health check-ups and more empathy on the part of adults and other children.

But back when a teacher referred me, it probably caused me more drama than help.

As I've mentioned before, I was practically a straight-A student. I didn't have many behavioral flaws, but as I got older, some of the deep-seated issues I never knew how to resolve broke through in a spectacular fashion.

Embedded in me was fury, and it was ready to come out as blind rage, given the right opportunity. In fifth grade, I snapped because of a journal assignment. We were asked to write a letter to someone from the point of view of a fictional character. I didn't think much about the actual assignment, so my subconscious took over. My letter was written from the perspective of a young, mixed-race boy whose father had left at some point in his youth, leaving his mother working on her own to raise a child. Another man stepped into the picture and began to physically and mentally abuse the boy, driving him to thoughts of suicide. The hypothetical boy climbed onto the Williamsburg Bridge and jumped to his hypothetical death.

Was it autobiographical? Well, let's say the only real hypothetical was the part about the death.

After I handed in the assignment, my mother was immediately notified and told that I would have to attend a few sessions in a psychiatry clinic. I wasn't told this was happening until I had to go—and the appointment carried a terrible stigma. Latino families often believe that mental illnesses are a direct reflection of parenting or proof of some kind of defect, both of which bring shame and humiliation. (I often wonder if the mental grit it took for our families to make it as far as we did is what makes us so resistant to treatment and discussing our wounds.)

Over four boring sessions, the psychiatrist tried everything she could to get me to open up, from warm and suggestive questions to computer games. No luck. I'm not sure if more sessions would have broken through my impenetrable defenses, but I never found out: my mom pulled me out before that could happen.

I was set free from the sessions but not the mental angst, which I carried for decades. A few years ago, my mother, brother, and I walked by that same clinic. I said, "Oh look, that's where I used to go." My brother didn't understand, but my mom sure did. She began to tell me the backstory of how I ended up there: a long meeting with the teacher and the principal, along with a few crying sessions. She told me that she had read the letter I'd written; until that moment, I believed she had never read it. She said she had been shocked, that she could not understand how the man she loved could have inspired her eldest child to write such a thing. She said the school kept it for documentation, as tears streamed down her face. She cries to this day recounting the story.

I walked ahead a little, knowing she had never had this conversation with the person who had inspired the letter to begin with: my stepfather. Then, I took a step back, trying my best to understand. In the short term, reporting these behaviors can tear families apart, attracting suspicion and bringing unwanted people into a home. For people whose incomes, apartments, and health are already constantly monitored, putting additional federal agencies on a family's case can add a lot more stress to a situation. Was it better to bring up the beatings and threats that occurred in my house when my mother wasn't looking? How much would I hurt my brother Ralf, who didn't know how much his father had hurt me? How could I make our weekly interactions less awkward? How could I forgive the hurt the way God asked me to in Mass and follow Jesus's example?

How was I supposed to know that writing a pseudo-fictional story would send me to psychiatric sessions on a regular basis, tuning the therapist out because I just wanted things to be normal?

In 1995, a couple of years after I wrote that letter, the news broke that a six-year-old Cuban girl by the name of Elisa Izquierdo had been beaten to death by her mother, Awilda Lopez, in their New York City apartment. There had been signs that Elisa was being abused, but too many people had looked the other way, unable to break their unspoken deference to parents on childrearing even when our children are beaten into compliance. Names like Nixzmary Brown and Ronnie Antonio Paris, children abused, beaten, murdered by their own families over the last two decades, still make my eyes twitch with fury, mainly because of situations where people felt uncomfortable trying to change a child's home situation. Children who had whole lives ahead of them, an opportunity to rise, instead become statistics.

This idea that snitches get stitches should make our community want to re-open those wounds and extract the evils festering beneath them. We have to move away from allowing distant authority figures to tell us how to run our families and develop stronger local networks, made up of people who can help alleviate our depression and hopelessness. Schools alone can't save kids from that. Neither can parents on their own. My mother did the best she could, but she didn't learn how to handle those situations. Stigmatizing kids who receive psychiatric help as weak perpetuates the behavior that causes them to need that help in the first place.

For all the dull lectures and trainings teachers receive as first responders to possible abuse and other problems, the fact is that many children are better off when the adults in their lives are encouraged to be alert toward symptoms of trouble at home. But as we move toward a more rigid focus on instruction, we force the personal to the side. If it is true, as many of my fellow educators like to say, that we are not just teaching English or math but teaching *children* these subjects, then we have to wake up to the need to restore a balance. A great formal education is not the only factor that matters.

Teachers try their hardest, but can't always "save" children from their desperate situations. The law mandates that teachers must report any indications that a child may have an issue at home, from black eyes and beaten faces to consistently smelly clothes. We can't always follow through with what happens next; the guidance counselor, dean, or principal handles that. A pile of paperwork gets filled out, parents get called in, and we are asked to trust the system.

To an extent, it makes sense to leave certain things to the professionals because that's their job. Teachers are supposed to focus mainly on students' academic situations. Veteran teachers always advise us to focus on our classrooms; we can't fight every battle. We have dozens of other students who need us at 100 percent as well. Trying to do too much for one student could take away from working for the eighty-nine other students who need our attentions.

But we cannot allow the most vulnerable kids to freeze themselves to the point where they don't share their pain. Like their parents before them, they will hold it inside instead of finding ways to cope with it—and then will lash out against the next generation. I'm not okay with that. Because snitches still get stitches—even if the wounds never get healed.

GOD GOT JOKES, SON

My first real classroom activity with eighth-graders was a complete failure. It was like stepping on your shoelaces while walking, having your knees buckle under you, and letting your face fall flat on a huge cream pie with a live studio audience waiting for you to say, "Did I do that?"

Idealist that I am, when I first strutted into the classroom, I thought I'd pick up a piece of chalk and automatically get the respect necessary to make the remaining 179 days left in the year smooth sailing. I chose an activity that I was certain would make these garrulous eighth-graders see themselves as mathematicians and scientists in no time. (After all, they were classified as "Alpha students," as in high achievers.) In retrospect, I should have stuck with Gary Rubinstein's *Reluctant Disciplinarian* and kept it simple and plain. This transformative teaching was much harder than I originally thought. I'm still wiping cream off my face.

The activity involved dividing the students into groups and giving each group a piece of chart paper. I then asked them to write down occupations in which math was absolutely necessary. When it came time to share what they came up with, almost every group responded with something that involved drugs—a synchronicity that cracked them up, but that bothered me deeply.

"Don't you all have high expectations?" I asked them. "Aren't you supposed to be Alpha students?" Azzam, the class clown, said, "Yeah, but just because we're Alpha students doesn't mean we're smart."

No, but he's definitely a smart-ass. *Smart-ass.* I wanted to respond just like that, but I had to let it go and wallow in the cream pie sticking to my goatee.

I realized I was going to have to reveal more of my personality, the one that had made it through decades of being surrounded by wannabe drug dealers and kleptomaniacs. I'd simply have to inject a little more sarcasm into my classroom persona. Then they would bow down to my humor and linguistic prowess and I would conquer them all.

But first, I'd try it on my seventh-graders.

Sometime around December, we were studying geometric figures when a young gentleman, a seventh-grade class clown, said to me, "Mr. Vilson, I bet you I can make you laugh."

"Okay . . ."

"Why was six afraid of seven? Because seven eight nine! Get it?" Mild chuckles followed, but not from me. If there was ever a time to get the class clown, it was here.

"Michael, that joke is older than World War II. That was wack!"

Just like that, my mask had come undone. The whole class cracked up. It was uproarious. Michael laughed along, but he also looked a bit like a walking stop sign. I felt bad for a second, but after that, I had his respect, as well as that of the rest of the class. Now they'd think twice before coming into my classroom with weak jokes. Ain't no half-steppin'.

The moment to get even with Azzam came a month later, when we were getting into the meat of eighth-grade math: transformations. By that point, I had called every one of my eighth-graders' parents at least twice and I hadn't cracked so much as a half-smile.

As a young Black/Latino male teacher, I often got the question, "So are you married?" Naturally, I would say, "Yes." And they'd say, "To who?"

"Her name is Math," I'd reply. "Now get back to work!"

They either laughed or rolled their eyes at their corny math teacher. But on this day, Azzam decided he'd test me further. Since his crack about Alpha students, he had consistently annoyed the hell out of me every chance he got. Even when he was doing well in class, I often had to call his house for some knuckleheaded thing he had done (or not done).

On this day he came up to me and said, "So, Mr. Vilson, guess what?"

"Yes, Azzam?"

"I was doing your wife last night. She was really good." The rest of the class laughed and stared at me, awaiting my reaction.

I furled my lower lip, nodding my head while everyone got their giggles in. Then I said:

"Funny you should say that, because I talked to my wife last night and she said you didn't do her very well."

"OHHHHHH!!!!" yelled the class.

The crowd went wild. I couldn't help but add, "That's why she came back to me." More giggles.

Azzam just hung his head and went back to work, thinking of a comeback at his desk. I probably went overboard, and I only slightly regret it.

(Actually, I don't, but I'll say I do just so people don't think I'm any less of an educator.)

After that, Azzam and I exchanged funny barbs for the rest of the year. The more ridiculous we became, the more I looked at him less as a student and more as a son.

Sarcasm violates one of Jon Saphier's tenets in *The Effective Teacher*, but humor tinged with sarcasm can go a long way. Students need to know that beneath that edifice of professionalism there's a human being who understands and can relate to them. Communicating this and learning how to play with it can take some experience. I've learned over the years that it's important to establish a direct and strong rapport with students in their first few months of class; nowadays, I keep most of my dialogue calculated and measured until we've gotten into a routine. Then I'll giggle at a joke.

I can sum up my rules as follows. If a student makes a funny joke:

Before they know the teacher: "Funny. Get back to work." Serious face. Deep breaths. Nod and don't get the kid in trouble unless the joke is highly offensive. If it's offensive, it's not funny. I repeat: Not funny.

After they know the teacher: "Oh, that was funny." Laugh for five or six seconds. "All right, that was good. Get back to work now." If it was really funny, walk away, because otherwise it will be a lost class.

Jokes can be a great unifier. But if they are taken too far, they can be used to embarrass and ostracize—a limit I crossed early on in my on-the-job teacher education. Yet, more often than not, the jokes my students and I share pull us closer to each other, including those on the receiving end of the joke.

What's funny is that, now, Azzam's got math under his skin. A promising mechanical engineer, he keeps in touch via Facebook. I know he's probably creating havoc for some professor out there. Math and I thank God for that every time we see him.

♦

I barely saw his mouth move, but the words coming out of it sounded like mine only a few years prior:

"José, you don't understand. This class is probably the worst I've seen. When it comes to classroom management, I'm good, but with this class? I got a kid who straight up comes to my face and says, 'Yo, so let's fight!' OUTTA NOWHERE! And what do I say?"

"Well?"

"I said, 'All right, then. Just know I'm not going to hit you.'"

"That's deep, my man."

"Hell yeah, but that's the thing; things are getting crazier by the day, so you know what I do? When the class gets in, I teach the five or so kids who really want to learn in the back of the room so they can work by themselves, and then, when everybody else is like, 'Yo, what are we learning?' I go around the room like that until most of the class works."

Right then, it clicked. For years, I was too embarrassed to discuss my miserable attempts at teaching one particular class, but here was Edgar, a friend whose work ethic, intellect, and cool demeanor I and many others admired. He had found his own rigorous pedagogy in difficult conditions. Outside the classroom, he was a committed father and husband and an inquisitive learner.

Inside that particular classroom, though, he could have been mistaken for a brand-new teacher—at least by someone who had never been in that situation. There are thousands of classes across the country that will refuse to bend or sway to the teacher's instructions, no matter what classroom management guide he or she picks up.

I still remember the first day my principal sat me down and showed me the roster for 702. I recognized a couple of students from the year before, but the rest were brand new to our school. He emphasized the fact that they came from a school with a culture of low expectations, even for its most gifted children. He then said that, based on my performance the previous year, I was probably the best fit for the class. Skimming the roster of state math and English scores, my eyes glistened with hope that this was the opportunity to be the transformative educator I had studied all summer to be, the Jaime Escalante I'd always aspired to be.

God got jokes.

After the first two weeks or so of class (the honeymoon period), the students' intellectual and behavioral flaws overcame me like a tidal wave—and I barely had a Hawaiian shirt on for cover. Not including the five students I'd taught previously, the students ran the gamut of what America might consider troubled: kids from group homes, kids who'd recently immigrated into the country, kids who barely spoke English, kids who tagged up entire desks right in front of substitute teachers, kids whose fathers sold drugs, kids whose parents barely came home, and kids classified with more acronyms than I care to recall.

I survived the next 150 days by attempting all kinds of strategies, which could have been compiled in a volume titled *Things to Do (and Not Do) in Your First Year as a Teacher*. For instance, I would try a lesson on my homeroom class; if it went reasonably well, I would tinker with it to make it easier to digest for the students in 702. After the requisite ten minutes it took to settle them down at the beginning of class, they finally would sit down and start writing. But the talking was absolutely incessant throughout my lesson and anything I could muster resembling a sequence of thoughts would fall apart. By the twenty-fifth minute of class, I just went straight to the kids who wanted me to teach and focused on presenting the lesson to them.

I made all kinds of mistakes: I was serious when I could have lightened up; I yelled when it wasn't required; I confronted kids I didn't need to; I joked when I should have clamped down; I didn't correct quizzes—or anything else for that matter—quickly enough. I didn't scare them enough into getting better grades. I didn't earn their respect consistently enough. I smiled before December.

When a fellow edublogger asked his followers on Twitter one day how often we blame ourselves for the things we bring and don't bring to the table as teachers, I said, "All. The. Time."

Some days, I could sneak in a really good lesson on scientific notation or graphing an equation and get all but one student relatively interested, and that would be an overwhelming success for me. Whenever anyone other than the usual suspects expressed a sense of curiosity, I ran to it immediately and tried to capitalize on it. Unfortunately, I couldn't get the curiosity to extend to other children. I was also constantly up against the culture of the previous school, never mind our own.

One reward I kept up my sleeve as an incentive for good behavior was use of the school's computer lab. I didn't trust most of the class with the classroom laptops, so I told them that if they behaved, I'd bring them to the lab. But it turned out I wasn't the first to think of this approach; our permanent substitute and other teachers were apparently doing the same thing, so what I thought would be a treat after they behaved for an entire day became a treat if they behaved for thirty minutes, twenty minutes, five minutes . . . I can't remember how many times I whispered "This can't be life" after taking them to those computer labs. I felt people watching me as I fell deeper down this hole, collecting evidence of my failures.

I had classes where I asked students to present their material despite never having taught them real presentation skills. (I could barely hold their attention myself!) The best part of this exercise was my policy of taking points off students' grades if they made any noise during some else's presentation. This saved me energy for a few days, but it was hardly a sustainable formula for quiet.

I wasn't alone in struggling with the class. The English teachers had tried partitioning it into two sections, which didn't help much; the science teacher resorted to throwing students out of the classroom; the math teacher found himself reconsidering his fantasies of having any increased leadership role in the building—or anywhere else.

Sometime in March, when things got really tough, I tried to arrange a meeting with administrators and deans. I wanted to be taught how to handle the situation, but instead, they used it against me in a schoolwide meeting about how teachers needed to address their own classroom problems.

God got jokes.

By April, I was actually thanking God for giving me the chance to grade the math state exams for an entire week and a half. When the acting principal sat me down a few weeks later, I honestly didn't know what to expect. Upon hearing that the position of math coach had opened up, I'd sent in my résumé. In June, the same man who had handed me 702's roster decided to relieve me of my classroom duties for the remainder of the year.

I knew he had his reasons for pulling me out, even as I secretly seethed that I hadn't gotten the chance to finish out the year. I knew he was right. It gave me a little more time to reflect on this brutal chapter in my life. It was also a chance to plot my revenge for next year—not against any one person, but against the idea that I couldn't teach.

God got jokes, and after a few years of holding the memories in, I would finally be able to laugh along.

"I DON'T WANT TO TALK
ABOUT PRIVILEGE. NOW HERE'S
MY GOOGLE GLASS."

I was having a conversation with an educator who worked at a school that has laptops for every child, readily available computer labs with fast, state-of-the-art equipment, wireless Internet access for all, and SMART Boards in every classroom. Teachers and other adults at the school saw themselves less as people using their expertise to guide students than as facilitators, live bodies just in case anything went wrong. The media, city and state politicians, and futurists alike had lauded the school for these advancements and often used it as a model for what was possible. The educator, too, appreciated the school because it put technology to which students would otherwise have limited access in the palms of their hands.

Yet it made him uncomfortable to know that the kids spent exorbitant amounts of time learning tech instead of actually *using* it. Instead of working with students on finding square roots, teachers had to work out the mandated programs' glitches for the first fifteen minutes of class before getting to the lesson. The more examples this teacher brought to the fore, the more we wondered whether members of this technological utopia, bereft of the complexities of a more human experience, could see it as part of the problem with education technology as a whole. I wondered how

the kids at that school must feel, knowing that they were function-
ing as robots in learning about robots.

As if tech itself replaces necessary pedagogy.

That's primarily my issue with the close-knit collective
dubbed "ed-tech." As a man who graduated with a degree in
computer science, I roll my eyes every time someone invokes the
term; half the time "ed-tech" is faux-expertise, a title used to
make someone look like they know something about technology
and education integration, regardless of whether they actually do.
Often they know diluted versions of both. In one egregious instance, a popular ed-techie asked his thousands of Twitter followers how to change a .lnk file into a workable video file—a basic
question that Google could probably have answered better than
I could in 140 characters. But I told him anyway. I felt terrible,
not because I had to tell him in a public forum, but because he's
out there telling the world he is a tech expert—and he is teaching
kids, too.

This speaks to the flimsy nature of current technology. Everyone needs to have all of the answers, do all of the things, be in all
of the conferences, and put all of it in their social-media profile,
even as they are learning along with the rest of us. The next new
thing's promoters promise it will transform learning, raise test
scores, assist with homework, make teachers' tiresome jobs easier,
and feed recommendations to administrators—all of this replica-
ble and supported throughout the implementing district. (As an
aside, this thing is also cost-effective as compared to the last new
thing, even when few learned how to fully implement the last
new thing.)

The more new things come out, the more techies who feign
relevance need to stay current— but to what end? If the students,
teachers, or parents don't actually see value in taking time to implement this new thing, why pretend expertise? As education
writer Audrey Watters reminds us, "Why have we been so keen for
so long to automate teaching and learning? What does this say

about our vision of the purpose, let alone the future of education?"* At the risk of sounding primordial, I would rather have a school that uses only pencil and paper but teaches its kids very well than a school equipped with a billion and one glittery doohickeys and thingamajigs that don't, in themselves, teach anything.

Why not be authentic? Why not say you're learning, just like the children must?

Furthermore, when companies license teachers to use their products, we end up tied to them for right or wrong. In 2013, the Los Angeles United School District deployed iPads for every child, with Pearson software preinstalled. When people first told me about it, I scoffed (in my mind). If kids can hack administrator passwords on school computers to install spammy software, what makes them think that a closed-source yet customizable iOS on an Apple product is sacred? In only a few weeks, the program got labeled a failure—not because the students didn't learn (debatable), but because they didn't learn the way the district wanted them to learn. They didn't follow its divine plans—ironic, since the Apple corporation had banked on its antiauthoritarian image ever since 1984, when it aired a commercial that showed an athlete throwing a sledgehammer into a huge, dystopian screen.

Thirty years later, we still want kids to "think different," yet we use tech to standardize them instead.

This is how we become walking advertisements for corporations willing to throw millions at educators to use their products exclusively with children—and hawk them to our students, as present and future consumers. People who only work within the boundaries of third-party vendors' instructions are projecting this framework around our students. To wit, much of what I've seen in ed-tech amounts to the value of a screensaver: entertaining and dazzling to the eye, but irrelevant to the task at hand.

---

* Audrey Watters, "Teaching Machines: The Drive to Automate Education," *Hack Education*, undated, http://teachingmachin.es.

The future of teaching isn't a place spliced from the fantasies of *The Matrix* and *Back to the Future*. I'd prefer it be a place where we value informed citizenry and authentic creativity, abstract reasoning and productive curiosity: things many of us only pretend to want for students. But the pressure for teachers to look impressive and dynamic is immense, and "ed-tech" is a useful gimmick for projecting a set of skills that could make you seem more qualified than the next teacher.

New York City has recently been mired in scandals about "blended learning," in which students take "credit recovery courses" online in lieu of actual high-school credits. In these classes, a student just logs on to his or her computer, watches a video from a virtual teacher, and answers a few questions from a quiz, with few criteria for demonstrating actual learning. A teacher's roster for supervising these periods might include hundreds of students; the bare minimum is to be present in the room. The adult in the room needn't even be licensed in the area in which the students are taking the course—just good enough to help with any technical issues. This is the opposite of what I and so many others envision as the future of integrating education with tech.

Some are doing it right. Blogger and professor Shelly Blake-Plock, an admitted ed-techie, integrates technology with pedagogy—but he doesn't use technology in spite of pedagogy. The latter is far more important than the former, and the former is a complement to the latter. Shelly also has an understanding of the real world, something missing among many of the ed-tech leaders at the forefront of this cultish movement. New York physics teacher Frank Noschese uses technology in a nifty way, waiting until the last, most necessary moments to use computers in his experiments. Jaymes Dec uses machines like 3-D printers to promote STEM (science, technology, engineering, and math) thinking at the all-girls Catholic Marymount School. In all three cases, their technology integrates almost seamlessly with their pedagogy, which is progressive and not lacking in content or difficulty.

As friend and *Edutopia* education blogger Mary Beth Hertz says,

> Before everyone goes and downloads a million apps or gets too excited about bright and shiny technology, it's important that teachers really think about whether bringing that app into the classroom will enhance or transform the learning. For instance, just because an app gives kids great practice on their math facts, does that mean that they should be doing it in class? Isn't that the same thing as handing out a worksheet and saying "practice!" instead of making the best use of your in-class time with them? What if they used the iPad to capture right angles in the classroom or to create visualizations of math problems? What if they wrote their own math problems, challenged each other to solve them, and then used an app that allowed them to record themselves solving the other person's problem? Not only could they document that classmate's success in creating a workable challenge, but they could also keep the video for other classmates to view and learn from.*

By contrast, there is another set of ed-techers who see tech as *the* element, as if constantly using the phrase "game-changer" shuffles the actual game or the players. They don't advocate well—if at all—for closing the "digital divide," a term to describe the socioeconomic factors that lead to the difference between rich and poor students in the way of technology. Smartphones have given a lot more people access to technology across different socioeconomic classes, but the speed and frequency still varies. So does the amount of professional development available to certain districts and teachers versus others. The nuance is missing from this conversation.

As long as you use the right jargon, have the right look, smile hard enough, go to the right conferences, and avoid any real conversation about race, culture, class, politics, or any kind of privilege, then you're a shoo-in for the clique. As we mindlessly follow

---

* Mary Beth Hertz, "Advice to New Technology Coaches," *Edutopia*, August 28, 2013, www.edutopia.org/blog/advice-to-new-technology -coaches-mary-beth-hertz.

these conversations without a resolute understanding of the true objective—educating our students—we lose out on some really deep talk. Using tech as some sort of false equalizer provides a shield for not discussing the stereotypical happy-go-lucky, mostly Caucasian, middle- to upper-income, male educators who rave about their pocket revolutions via their preferred social networks.

If we step too far out of bounds, throats clench and shrugs take over.

Don't worry, though. Keep having your big meetings, gadgets and fancy doohickeys at the ready. You can most certainly Google Glass, but you can't Google "class." Cool.

WE DON'T NEED NO EDUCATION

In January 2011, I had the pleasure of attending EduCon 2.3, a national conference in Philadelphia. The annual event is held at the Science Leadership Academy (SLA), a magnet school with a diverse student body that partners with Philadelphia's Franklin Institute. The school is devoted to project-based learning and student-centered initiatives—in laymen's terms, pretty cool stuff. The SLA's founding principal is Chris Lehmann, who, along with social-studies super-pedagogue Diana Laufenberg, welcomed attendees with warmth and camaraderie. The conference was filled with edu-lebrities and edu-nerds (I'm either/or, depending on the day) and it felt appropriate—and rare—for us to convene not in a large convention hall, but in a school.

The conference itself is conversation-based, meaning Chris doesn't necessarily want lectures but discussion and debate, including on the difficult stuff. Upon arriving, my fiancée and I went to a session with elementary-school principal George Couros and Chris. The topic at hand was the concept of "inquiry," a word I despise because of what it has become in my district.

I want my kids to learn how to question effectively, and inquiry-based education certainly promotes this if it is done correctly. But in my experience, "inquiry" often means a bunch of teachers looking at a handful of students and trying to fix them. When people use the word "inquiry" in the NYC Department of Education, it usually refers to an "inquiry team" dedicated to working with a

143

small subset of students on a specific skill. The team meets on a regular basis—weekly is common—and identifies a particular weakness of their lowest-performing students in a given class. The skills can range from vocabulary use to numeracy, but it's usually something with which every teacher of a particular class sees the students struggling. It sounds like an effective practice—except, the way it plays out in public schools, it doesn't really lead to a real change in practice. It works for some schools, given the right conditions, but it's generally done as a matter of compliance, not as a tool for real collaboration and discussion.

"Inquiry" in this workshop, by contrast, meant asking good questions throughout the learning process, so naturally I was curious.

Before the conversation started, though, I wanted a little snack to quiet my grumbling stomach. The library had potato chips. Mmm. Potato chips.

In the library I encountered a group of young ladies of color wearing lab coats and bright smiles. One of them looked at me and whispered, "Well, there's one."

Here we go.

I asked them, with a mischievous grin, "So what exactly were you ladies counting?" They tried to change the topic, but I knew already.

As I surveyed the library, I picked up on what they had noticed: that the minute I walked into the library, I represented the entirety of EduCon's racial diversity. The students came from all walks of life, many from neighborhoods some of the participants drive by swiftly. I tried to make some small talk with them to dig a little further, but they already knew that I knew what they knew and gave bland answers so as not to offend the passersby. I bid them adieu and went to the conversation.

The discussion included George and Chris, along with a number of teachers, principals, and other ed specialists who went back and forth about different models of inquiry-based schooling. Inquiry-based schooling is the ideal model for progressive educators, ones who believe children should learn mainly through interests. Schools should have flexible schedules and structures and teachers should ask students what they want to learn in a particular course of study.

The most recent famous example of this is Sugata Mitra's experiment with computers in the 1990s. He left computer access open to children in impoverished neighborhoods in India. Rather than destroy the technology, kids started to learn how it worked, learning everything from the English language to DNA replication.* In schools across the world, progressive leaders like Deborah Meier have built schools with this mindset, hoping to spur creativity in different capacities. There are limits to this type of education, including funding and school systems, but the conversation steered participants to discuss how they try to implement it in their schools. One gentleman in the conversation pointed out, "Well, that might be great for some kids. But some others might need direct instruction."

I blinked a bit; I'm not afraid of speaking my mind in these environments, but first I had to feel out the room. Before I could even let out a word, Chris responded, and I'll do my best to quote him here:

"Well, I'd be careful with that, because when people hear that, then we start getting into whose kids should get inquiry-based school, and it means that we inevitably run into issues of race, class, and gender. I know that if enough of the Black boys started asking the hard questions, they'd probably feel like getting a gun." Collective gasp. Except for two of us. Luz nodded and I smirked. "And not so that they'd shoot another Black kid, but so they could run up to City Hall and ask 'What's going on?'"

After he said it, I imagined my students running up to Gracie Mansion singing Pink Floyd's "Another Brick in the Wall (Part

---

* Joshua Davis, "How a Radical New Teaching Method Could Unleash a Generation of Geniuses," *Wired*, October 15, 2013, www.wired.com/business/2013/10/free-thinkers.

II)'': *We don't need no education*. Chris succinctly analogized the ways in which we tell certain children how they can be educated versus how others *must* be educated. Was inquiry-based education not good enough for children in inner Philly? If not, should they ask other types of questions of their government officials about their conditions? The gun reference seemed to shock an otherwise mollified audience into one that had to confront its privilege.

Inquiry-based education only for the ones society felt could handle it wasn't good enough.

Amazed at Chris's acute response to a seemingly benign question, I scanned the room. Walking the halls at SLA, I had counted with one hand the number of adult participants of color versus the many students of color. Things like this usually don't faze me, but it drove home the reasons why my work is important. People of color are rarely represented at these events, and those with the leverage or popularity to highlight that problem rarely do so in their own spheres. Instead they wait for another person of color to acknowledge the problem in their private quarters.

I decided to speculate about this problem openly with my friends. I asked some of the friends I had at the conference, "What are we going to do about this? Philly has all these teachers of color and they can't get access to this?" Some of my friends agreed but didn't have solutions. Diana said, point-blank, that they had done some outreach to the local schools but that she honestly didn't know what she could do above that. Chris pointed back to some of my blog posts about integration versus segregation, which only made me feel more conflicted.

On the one end, Martin Luther King Jr.'s dream meant every child in this country would find well-resourced schools open to them, with access to the curriculum that opened the doors of the middle and upper echelons of society to their white peers. Yet integration felt forced, foisted upon people in a few different circles. Even with separate and unequal facilities, some people of color saw an excellent opportunity to teach the unspoken histories of the United States, ones currently deemed too radical for standards and standardized testing. How many of us on any side of the racial spectrum believe in true integration, the type that demands we acknowledge our differences and work through them? Or do we believe that white kids, and a "talented tenth" of every other racial group, should get the type of education promoted at SLA while everyone else gets to do their own thing in another corner?

As someone who has spurred on discussions about education, am I obligated to bring up race when others in this community refuse to? Sure looks like it. I surely wouldn't want to create my own sphere that isolates our people per se, but, similar to the NFL's Rooney Rule (which requires the league to interview minority candidates for senior positions), I'd have to promote fellow educators of color in ways they're probably not used to.

No, I don't want to run around reminding my fellow edunerds of their commensurate whiteness, nor do I feel the need to constantly discuss our most racially underrepresented and socially disadvantaged children. My presence at these conferences alone reminds them just fine. Plus, I'm sure to hear replies of "Well, I know how you feel because my grandparents went through these struggles," rather than, "There's a problem. Let's fix it." The first condescends; the second empathizes.

The problem isn't just at EduCon, TEDx conferences, or any other particular event; it's endemic in education and technology. Few people of color in the small world of the edu-blogosphere get called upon to opine on education on the same levels and platforms to which many white educators get access, and I appreciated Chris's blunt and direct approach to the question. He's obviously dealing with challenges of racial representation at his school every day. After the conference ended, I decided to write a post entitled, "#EduCon, Edu-Nerds, Chris Lehmann, and a Slice of Race in the 21st Century," hoping to spark a conversation about race in education spaces, but also to highlight what Chris had to say to people who otherwise didn't want or need to deal with race at all.*

Chris replied to my post with this:

It is very important to me to attempt to be an ally in the fight for a more just society, but I recognize fully that when I speak about issues of race, I speak as a white, male educator, and thus my role is "ally" and there are those who can and do speak with a deeper, more personal connection to the struggle than I can ever have. The first time I had to catch a cab for one of my students of color in NYC over fifteen years ago hammered that home.

. . . I think it is incredibly important that the chorus of voices saying the kinds of things that I said must be diverse— that is the role of allies. But there is [a] subtle and powerful and necessary difference between saying that I was "speaking for you" which I could never and would never presume to do but instead, in that moment, "speaking so you don't have to." . . . It is my way of trying to make sure that it doesn't always have to be a teacher of color who calls racial issues while remaining powerfully aware of how much I am still learning in this sphere.

It is a huge challenge for me, and to even attempt it is to attempt to speak with a combination of conviction and humility that can seem nearly impossible. It is a fine line, to be sure— one I've screwed up before and, sadly, will screw up again. But it is an internal struggle that, to me, is worth having, and it was very much on my mind. I'm pretty sure I looked over at you when I was done with a look of "That didn't suck, right?"

And I don't want anyone thinking that the only reason it mattered that José was in the room was because he is of color. It is because he is The José Vilson, poet, teacher, writer, thinker, friend and Black/Latino activist, because, as I have learned from some of the incredible teachers of color who have taken the time to mentor me in my role as a white teacher/principal in the diverse schools I have worked, we are never just one thing, we are always all that we are, and what I was aware of was that there was someone in the room whose views and writings and thoughts about race, education and "race and education" had

---

* This chapter is derived from and expounds upon that blog post.

powerfully and deeply influenced my own.

I'll end with this. We have to find ways to make EduCon more diverse. . . . We have work to do. I am proud, humbled, honored to feel like I can do that work alongside you.

What a *mensch*.

The critical part of Chris's point: doing it so I didn't have to.

After some time, I wondered why people at the conference and in my daily interactions in education spheres thought the immediacy of ed-tech mattered more than ameliorating race relations in this country. Do SMART Boards and iPads really change pedagogy for the millions of students institutionally ostracized based on their race, religion, or gender? Or are they merely Band-Aids that can be used to say, "Oh look, we did something and we never had to get our hands dirty to make it happen"? I also know that, ultimately, one can't force others to change their behaviors; they have to believe in that change.

When discussing race, the conversation always starts off rather well; people get their opinions heard. Yet the people most privileged by the racial construct often find ways to disassociate themselves from the conversation, walking away slowly, gulping down guilt.

Three years later, in 2014, Audrey and I led a discussion on privilege at EduCon 2.6—now more diverse in attendance and thought, having graduated from the silo that excludes discussions of race, class, and gender. It was prompted by a plethora of incidents that had happened in a year's span: the classification of Seattle Seahawks player Richard Sherman as a "thug," educational theorist Grant Wiggins's liberal use of the word "apartheid," the acquittal of child-murderer George Zimmerman, Secretary of Education Arne Duncan's dismissal of suburban white moms in the education-reform debate (and the perpetual dismissal of urban mothers of color), Richie Incognito's apparent carte blanche in the Miami Dolphins' locker room to berate Jonathan Martin in any way he pleased (including calling him a nigger), Questlove's open struggle with covert racism, Dylan Byers's rebuttal of Ta-Nehisi Coates's declaration that MSNBC show host Melissa Harris-Perry was America's foremost public intellectual, and what felt like weekly discussions about *who* ought to have the mic on any number of educational issues.

Needless to say, I was nervous about bringing this conversation to a place that, three years beforehand, had barely been able to handle Chris Lehmann's off-color commentary.

Our session was the most widely discussed conversation at the conference—and one of its most controversial. It also exceeded our wildest expectations. We had created a safe space for educators of all backgrounds to speak on the -isms face to face, without a limit of 140 characters. Everyone participated. Everyone expounded. It didn't matter whether the person had ten Twitter followers or forty thousand; everyone took part. Instead of expressing disappointment through back channels, educators and allies of all colors got to air their frustrations in a way that re-energized their work as they made their way back home.

Courageous are those who can stand in the conversation with a spirit of collaboration and understanding. It's important for us to critique, but just as important to find solutions. We can't solve the problems by ignoring them; we'll simply continue to promote them.

I believe we can do it so much better together.

Part Three

WHY YOU POST-RACIALISTS
GET IT WRONG . . . AGAIN

"They're doing that thing again," racially underrepresented people in this country whispered to themselves a few years back, when news broke out that the more than two hundred instances of the word "nigger" would be replaced by the word "slave" in a new edition of *The Adventures of Huckleberry Finn.* "Of the hundred things on our list that need improvement in this country for racial relations," we thought, "you chose THAT?!"

Erasing the N-word from one of the American literary canon's biggest children's books is akin to erasing the "three-fifths" representation of slaves from the US Constitution. Books, whether biographical or fictional, document our history. By deciding to use that language in his book, Mark Twain shone a light on the customs and history of his time, no matter how deplorable we consider them today. When we try to erase history, we beg our society to repeat the mistakes of its past. If we erased the "three-fifths," someone with little knowledge of US history could make a more profound case that the Constitution did, in fact, apply to every single person living in the United States, not strictly older, white, upper-class, Protestant males (despite the abundance of evidence to the contrary).

The same year that the controversy broke over the new edition of *Huckleberry Finn,* the state of Arizona instituted a set of directives against certain segments of educational curricula in the state. This bill followed the already tenuous relationship between the state government and underrepresented people in Arizona. Media reports about the bill called it a "ban on ethnic studies," which was deeply misleading. In fact, the ramifications went much further. Reading this bill, I noticed the language in Subsection A:

A. A SCHOOL DISTRICT OR CHARTER SCHOOL IN THIS STATE SHALL NOT INCLUDE IN ITS PROGRAM OF INSTRUCTION ANY COURSES OR CLASSES THAT INCLUDE ANY OF THE FOLLOWING:
1. PROMOTE THE OVERTHROW OF THE UNITED STATES GOVERNMENT.
2. PROMOTE RESENTMENT TOWARD A RACE OR CLASS OF PEOPLE.
3. ARE DESIGNED PRIMARILY FOR PUPILS OF A PARTICULAR ETHNIC GROUP.
4. ADVOCATE ETHNIC SOLIDARITY INSTEAD OF THE TREATMENT OF PUPILS AS INDIVIDUALS.*

Compare that to the language of this piece a few sentences down (Subsections E and F):

E. THIS SECTION SHALL NOT BE CONSTRUED TO RESTRICT OR PROHIBIT:
1. COURSES OR CLASSES FOR NATIVE AMERICAN PUPILS THAT ARE REQUIRED TO COMPLY WITH FEDERAL LAW.
2. THE GROUPING OF PUPILS ACCORDING TO ACADEMIC PERFORMANCE, INCLUDING CAPABILITY IN THE ENGLISH LANGUAGE, THAT MAY RESULT IN A DISPARATE IMPACT BY ETHNICITY.
3. COURSES OR CLASSES THAT INCLUDE THE HISTORY OF ANY ETHNIC GROUP AND THAT ARE OPEN TO ALL STUDENTS, UNLESS THE COURSE OR CLASS VIOLATES SUBSECTION A.
4. COURSES OR CLASSES THAT INCLUDE THE

---

* Arizona House Bill 2281, signed by Governor Jan Brewer on May 11, 2010, available at www.azleg.gov/legtext/49leg/2r/bills/hb2281s.pdf.

DISCUSSION OF CONTROVERSIAL ASPECTS OF HISTORY.

F. NOTHING IN THIS SECTION SHALL BE CONSTRUED TO RESTRICT OR PROHIBIT THE INSTRUCTION OF THE HOLOCAUST, ANY OTHER INSTANCE OF GENOCIDE, OR THE HISTORICAL OPPRESSION OF A PARTICULAR GROUP OF PEOPLE BASED ON ETHNICITY, RACE, OR CLASS.*

The authors of the legislation clearly tried to include language that would confuse people into thinking the bill doesn't bolster the legacy of the dominant culture in this country. But it fails the logic test, something I'm sure the lawmakers let happen on purpose.

For instance: how can a class specifically addressing Chicano/a culture not be designed in one way or another for pupils of a particular ethnic group, who identify with it? In teaching students about the legacy of César Chávez and Dolores Huerta, a teacher might inadvertently find him- or herself violating Subsection A: students may well feel a sense of ethnic solidarity and a desire to advocate on its behalf; students may feel resentment toward a race or class of people, given the oppression of their own people; students who are radicalized by that history might even find themselves whipped into a revolutionary fervor and wish to overthrow the United States government.

Even the word "might" might not be enough.

After all, once a community empowers its members to consider their own history as well as that of other underrepresented people, they will inevitably ask questions. Why did the Black Panthers organize in the face of oppression? Why did John Lennon's message of peace put him in the crosshairs of the FBI? Why aren't Frederick Douglass and John Brown considered as central to discussions of slavery in this country as Abraham Lincoln? If nothing in this bill restricts or prohibits the instruction or discussion of controversial topics in the history of the United States, then wouldn't the discussion of

---

* Ibid.

these groups and figures have to violate Subsection A in at least two out of four ways?

Unless, of course, this law prohibits actual discussion. Then this bill should state that, when discussing these topics, the teacher should read a few prescribed facts, sugarcoat them, perhaps say something like "I went through this struggle, too" with no deep comparison or contrast, then give a multiple-choice test using a narrow set of vocabulary taught beforehand. That's how I learned history for the majority of my schooling.

I also question the alarmist use of the word "overthrow." What this is actually intended to do is to preserve the status quo, to ensure the dominant culture's perpetual dominance. Teaching alternative narratives that tell the stories of oppressed groups is a way of challenging official narratives—and that is why it is so dangerous to the writers of this kind of law. To prevent solidarity between those of us desperately seeking to understand our identities in the American context, lawmakers create bills that ensure division and directly peg those who seek community as anti-American. This is not merely a ban on ethnic studies; it's a ban on education progress beyond the status quo. That's a crime within itself.

Which brings me back to *Huckleberry Finn*. On some level, I get it. The word "nigger" is not often used, aside from in a certain cultural context and in pop culture as a reflection of communities of color. Some whites still use it in a derogatory way, but many have also gotten a pass. The word and its history are rather complex— and that's why I would prefer it remain in the text. It opens the door to precisely the discussion the legislators in Arizona are trying to silence. Maybe it'll push us to keep having these discussions and stop acting like this never happened.

That is, assuming the teacher in charge has the racial consciousness to help his or her students navigate this historical terrain.

If not, maybe I don't want it taught.

Maybe.

HOW TO DROP THE MIC

Forecasts said the temperature would reach 100°F on Saturday, July 30, 2011, the day of the first-ever Save Our Schools (SOS) march in Washington, DC. I wouldn't have missed this for anything, though; when I received the invitation to speak in February, it was a matter of how, not if. Sponsored mainly by grassroots groups and eventually supported by local and national unions, SOS's conference and culminating march to the White House Ellipse urged political leaders to pursue education reform that focuses more on whole-child initiatives and less on school shutdowns and heightened, one-way accountability. I understood the urgency of fighting for equality for my students and against high-stakes testing, but I had an added responsibility to speak out about the lack of teachers' voices in creating policy.

I told John "Chance" Acevedo, a gifted poet and one of my teacher friends, about the event. The lineup featured speakers included Diane Ravitch (NYU professor), Jonathan Kozol (author, *Savage Inequalities*), Ceresa Smith (parent, National Board Certified teacher, renowned activist), Monty Neill (executive director of the nonprofit National Center for Fair and Open Testing, or FairTest), Angela Valenzuela (professor/activist), Linda Darling-Hammond (world-renowned Stanford University education professor), Pedro Noguera (NYU professor), Nancy Carlsson-Paige (educator, professor, activist), and some guy named Matt Damon. And me.

Chance cracked up. "Yo, that's like the 1927 Yankees and some guy from the Pee Wee leagues!" ("Oh man! At least give me

Robinson Canó!" I said.) I definitely didn't have the credentials the other speakers had, but I knew that when I came up to bat I'd get a solid hit out to center field. I belong.

As the march approached, so did testing season. Every meeting, conversation, professional development session, and system-wide email felt like a tap on the shoulder reminding us to pick up the pace. Meetings across the city centered on how best to address student weaknesses using standards-based assessments.

In other words: we're teaching to the test and we're not even trying to hide it.

I do emphasize "we." Even though I knew better than to buy into the testing model, I also felt chills every time I heard about the teacher data reports (TDRs). Teacher data reports rank teachers based on their students' test scores over one year's time and multiple periods, then uses those scores as a percentile to indicate how well we did compared to our colleagues. I feigned nonchalance to my colleagues, and I had enough evidence of my teaching to dissuade others from thinking otherwise, but these TDRs became the talk of the town: people have grown to equate a number with a fact. I was unnerved at the thought of another set of students not doing well on the math test and not graduating as a result. As the math coach, I also had lots to prove—not just to my fellow math teachers but also to the rest of the school. As the big tests approached, administrators and teachers alike felt increased pressure to perform.

New York schools chancellors changed, from Joel Klein to Cathie Black to Dennis Walcott, but very little changed about how we as a school were held accountable, even as the higher-ups played musical chairs with Mayor Bloomberg's favorites. After Bloomberg secured mayoral control for his schools and named antitrust prosecutor Joel Klein chancellor, Klein transformed the country's largest public school system by stuffing charter schools into public school buildings, increasing the local stakes for students, teachers, and parents via standardized test scores, and shaving off union power by stomping on seniority rights and creating reassignment centers.

These are the Department of Education's holding facilities, where more than six hundred teachers accused of misconduct or ostracized for legal or budgetary reasons were paid to work full-time, doing nothing for months or years at a time while awaiting resolution of their cases, as part of a wayward deal struck between then-chancellor Joel Klein and the teachers' union. Among those familiar with the NYC school system, they are referred to as "rubber rooms," an analogy to asylums. The city had thirteen reassignment centers until the practice was ended in 2010. These spaces became symbols of the waste and mistrust Klein engendered during his tenure as chancellor.

When Klein left the department to start up an education data-mining company named Amplify (and eventually become FOX founder Rupert Murdoch's consigliere), the appointment of publishing magnate Cathie Black only exacerbated the public perception of Michael Bloomberg as an out-of-touch one-percenter who looked out for his buddies by putting the least qualified people in his cabinet. At the end of Black's ninety-five-day tenure, Dennis Walcott took over as the head honcho. He didn't have much experience with education prior to being hired as deputy mayor of education in 2002, but by the time he was appointed as chancellor in 2011, he had the qualifications.

Despite the obvious bedlam at the district's central offices, Bloomberg made New York City feel like this was all part of the plan; anyone in the way—parent, student, or teacher—was a nuisance meddling in business that had nothing to do with them. He presided over press conferences the way kings preside over inquisitive minions, rolling his eyes whenever a journalist asked a question. The constant reorganization probably made protesting harder; one does not simply deconstruct an ever-changing structure.

Then there was the cumulus cloud of the Common Core State Standards (CCSS), which rose rapidly over NYC and the rest of the country in February 2011. In its continued attempts to remain at the forefront of education reform, the New York State Department of Education decided to "encourage" schools to begin adopting the CCSS, even as it kept the New York State Learning Standards in place as its official measuring stick for school success. Those of us in pilot schools worked with two sets of standards: one for the present, one for the future. The NYS and CCSS Standards would both show up in some way on the big tests, and we had to prepare students for this or else. As a collective, we barely got the right training, and couldn't discard the old standards to gain enough time to soak in the new standards.

An intelligent observer might think it would be wise to exempt schools from new accountability measures until 2014, the year schools would have to fully implement the CCSS, or that they would show up without interruption on the new tests. Instead, New York subjected schools to two different sets of standards and held us accountable to both.*

The English Language Arts and Math tests were administered in May. Soon thereafter, my younger brother graduated from Syracuse University. Overwhelmed with excitement for him and his classmates, I found myself deeply reflective about the current state of our schools. A couple of these graduates came from the same neighborhoods as my students. While I knew that college might not be for everyone, I started to feel more strongly that children of color have no reason not to go to college in the same numbers as white kids.

Fueled by this thought—along with the recently deceased Gil Scott-Heron's "Comment #1" off Kanye West's "Who Will Survive in America?"—I started to write the first draft of a poem, entitled "This Is Not a Test." Fury rang in my ears as I thought about the millions of students subjected to a two-hour test with so much power to decide their future. When school systems use *only* high-stakes tests to determine things like school funding, graduation cri-

---

* As it turns out, Pearson designed the 2013 New York State tests to align fully with the CCSS, bumping up the schedule about a year before we could have a chance to fully acclimate. We found out the standards contained in the exams sometime in late November, about a third of the way through NYS-aligned pacing calendars and units.

teria, and teacher evaluation, the pressure to perform often falls more on the student than anyone else. Countdowns, test-prep rallies, and preparation brochures reinforce this undue pressure. Whether all this consternation makes them more or less prepared for their future colleges and careers is left to be determined. Plus, I wanted to find a voice that sounded less like what I heard in the teachers' lounge and more like a teacher standing outside the government's door demanding answers for his students. I wanted to prove that teachers' voices could at once inspire and rebel. I wanted to speak in the rhythm of this burgeoning groundswell. I wanted to rip down the silos too many of us had created for ourselves.

A month before the Save Our Schools march and conference, which would feature a plethora of progressive professors, parent organizations, students, union officials, and activist-educators from across the country—I was struggling to get my thoughts together due to a maelstrom of professional development sessions and unanticipated conferences. Along with a few other people from my school, I got a chance to go to the education technology–focused Curriculum21 conference in Saratoga Springs, New York. Surely, no one would bring up high-stakes testing here. Anti-testing sentiments tend to come from folks who see themselves as political activists and, at the time, ed-techies preferred to step away from politically critical analyses of high-stakes testing.

Except I was wrong. Thank God.

In session after session, people shared their concerns about our schools' narrowing curriculum and state and federal administrations' lack of professional empathy. Ordinary teachers were speaking up in Hawaii, Arizona, and Pennsylvania as well as at this conference. My ears hummed with excitement. I encountered the same refrains when I went to Orlando, Florida, for the GE Developing Futures in Education conference a week before the SOS march.[*] Teachers

---

[*] According to its website: "The GE Foundation Developing Futures™ in Education Summer Conference brings together teachers, administrators and community members from school districts across the United States to foster

and principals shared their concerns about these accountability measures with David Coleman, consultant and head architect of the
CCSS, and other representatives from Student Achievement Partners,
the nonprofit consulting company that supports CCSS work. They
assured us they had created the best product possible. As we heard
representatives from the Smarter Balanced Assessment Consortium
and Partnership for Assessment of Readiness for College and Careers
(PARCC), the consortia responsible for creating the Common Core
assessments, attempting to clarify their stances on assessment, I
thought, *No matter how well-intentioned the CCSS might be, the administration of the assessments in practice could not live up to its vision.*

My anger was further fueled by a conversation I overheard at
the GE conference in which a teacher representative said about public schools, "Why would anyone teach in such horrible conditions?"

Whenever I hear things like this from the mouths of people
who ostensibly represent teachers, it enrages me. First, this attitude
assumes that the average teacher who works in these schools
shouldn't work there, even while also acknowledging the despica-
ble conditions under which so many of our students have to learn.
If it's hard for a teacher to work there, how hard did this representative think it felt for the students?

There's a certain age—around the same age at which the government mandates that students respond to their education via
Scantron—when their once-optimistic eyes become glassy, clouded
by the barriers standing in the way of their futures.

Thus I arrived at the place where I had been all along: believing that the change we seek in education must come from the people in the school building.

Those of us with enough voice and writing talent get the opportunity to reach a lot of people, both through the Internet and
in person, but most educators haven't gravitated toward expressing

---

new connections and preparations for the school year ahead" (GE Foundation,
"Education Conferences," undated, www.gefoundation.com/developing
-futures-in-education/education-conferences/).

themselves this way. Our jobs discourage vocalizing dissent, both through individual administrators' intimidation tactics and through formal Internet policies. The hours teachers spend in class and on paperwork also leave little energy for advocacy or political action. The Save Our Schools march was a chance to change this.

As I thought about the words I would share with the crowd, I settled on a metaphor that felt useful for articulating the problem as I saw it. When it comes to designing the policies that affect them and their students the most, teachers are less like architects and more like contractors, tasked with implementing someone else's plans as best we can. Why shouldn't we get more opportunities to build from our own vision of what education should look like?

On the Wednesday before the march, I posted my poem for my friends to read on my blog. A few people had seen it by then and given me constructive feedback, but it was only the next day that I actually read it aloud. I went through it a few times on the Amtrak train, but never really loudly. It wasn't until the night before the march that I performed the poem for an audience of two: my fiancée and our unborn child. Fellow writer Ynanna Djehuty had said I should spit it like a hard rap, and in that moment I saw the humor in some of what I had written a few weeks back.

Luz said, "It doesn't sound like you."

"What do you mean?"

"You sound like you're holding back. Remember: you're representing a big movement. You want to show the world that this matters to you, and how you represent it matters."

"OK, OK, OK."

I took a few breaths and reread it in a clear, solid voice. She nodded in approval. I scribbled notes on the poem, emphasizing some breaks, reminding myself to find a good, accessible pace. She said she felt the baby kick. She gassed me up pretty good.

The next day, I paced around the VIP tent as cameras circled Diane Ravitch, Jonathan Kozol, Deborah Meier, Ceresa Smith, and . . . Matt Damon, who had rushed out to Washington in the middle of filming the movie *Elysium* to speak with us. I also had my moments to chat with some of the speakers. The tent was buzzing with people waving their credentials, politicking and nudging their way into press stories. Some tried to make the case for why their positions were more important than others; others hovered over the refreshments.

Reason TV, the market-driven, libertarian media outlet, interviewed Damon for a video that shortly went viral. The reporter managed to get him fired up about his pro–public school stance, which further solidified his integrity with the rest of us. He caught some heat for telling the interviewer this:

> So you think job insecurity is what makes me work hard? I want to be an actor. That's not an incentive. That's the thing: See, you take this MBA-style thinking, right? It's the problem with ed policy right now, this intrinsically paternalistic view of problems that are much more complex than that. It's like saying a teacher is going to get lazy when they have tenure. A teacher wants to teach. I mean, why else would you take a shitty salary and really long hours and do that job unless you really love to do it?*

I didn't find his words any more valuable than those spoken by parents, students, and educators who came to the march, but his opinion mattered so much *because* it supported us. A few reporters from the *Christian Science Monitor, Washington Post,* and *Education Week* tried to capture the buzz with mostly positive reviews, upending the negative attention from critics who said that the march didn't offer any solutions.

Of course not. It's a march, not a policy meeting. Moving on.

After watching Richard Dreyfuss and *The Daily Show's* Jon Stewart surprise the audience with pre-recorded remarks, I heard slam poet Taylor Mali reciting "What Teachers Make" on stage while I quietly rehearsed on my own in the back. Mali's poem

---

* "ReasonTV" (YouTube user), "What We Saw at the Save Our Schools Rally in Washington D.C.," posted July 30, 2011, www.youtube.com/watch?v =TJ7icVvDK9I.

takes readers through a teacher's rant after someone at his dinner table makes a snide remark about his salary. When I first heard it I found it inspirational, a call to appreciate what educators do on a daily basis, and his words resonated with me long before I even knew I wanted to be a teacher. But this crowd wanted something more, a call to action that put our angst and agita about the corporatist takeover of schools. The congregation had come here to address and redress—and I needed to speak to that.

I sat down and tried to tune into my inner teacher.

I sought what my friend and educator Alexa Muñoz calls "the rage," that part of your heart that yells back at people or ideas that conflict with what you feel to be true or right. It's when you have an eighth-grade English language learner who is subjected to more than a test a week from April through June just in order to graduate. It's when you hear the president claim to appreciate educators of all stripes while reinforcing ideas from the previous administration, an administration that was supposed to be much worse on education issues. It's when you decide, for once, to take the culmination of struggle and indignation and mold it into electricity, the type of energy that sparks ideas and lights up classrooms at once. It's when you give your one spectacular speech in the classroom that you've saved for just the right occasion, the lull when students don't work to their fullest potential, the speech that sets the stage for you to catch your second wind for the second half of the school year.

Lupe Fiasco calls this an "inner G." *The Last Dragon* endowed it onto Taimak for the legendary "glow."

I sat at the foot of the stage for about fifteen minutes, hearing the other speakers but so tuned out that I barely noticed who would join the stage with me: Pedro Noguera and FairTest's Bob Schaeffer. Noguera's work with children of color had made him famous across the nation, particularly in New York City, where he consistently and publicly disagreed with the direction of the public schools during the Bloomberg era. His independence as a researcher might have rubbed a few lefties the wrong way, but his presence at the march that year made a believer out of me. I saw how deeply he cares for kids and for the struggle we've undertaken for better schools.

I took a few deep breaths, nervous to be among so many people whose work I admired, people who had never heard of me, people who only knew me from my blogging. Luz.

I regained my composure the minute I tapped the mic and said, "Testing, testing, one, two. . ." The audience let out a few giggles. A brisk wind rustled my pages and moved the sweat from my squinting eyes. The audience hummed, not knowing what to expect. I let the hum take over.

Whatever that energy was, I had simmered in its brew for about half an hour, and when the time came, I was ready to erupt.

This Is Not a Test

Welcome, America, to the latest installment of a people's
     march
For the next three minutes, I will ask you to defy protocol
Disband the status quo
Bust open these deformed gates
Unlock the teachers' lounge
Unlock the teachers' lounge
Unlock the teachers' lounge
I beg your pardon, but I am not your proctor
I march with the protestors, and our hands are raised,
A pledge for a new narrative
This is not a test!
This is not a test, Mr. President.
This is an assessment written against the idea that the
     dates and places of our history
Can be shrunk to the choice between B and C
And that is our purpose for this assembly
An extended response to a failed corporatist agenda
A reflection on the state of our most public of options

Measured through the rubric of human rights
But this is not a test!
This is not a test, Mr. Duncan
Take note: this is not us asking
This is not us begging
This is not us pleading
This is us fighting for all things equal
This is us uniting as a more perfect union
This is us reminding America of a promissory note
    unpaid
This is us writing our own documentation when
    politicians refuse our kids the opportunity
We are all DREAMers, and this is not a test!
This is not a test, Mr. Bloomberg
This is the generation of children from the classrooms
    where teachers boldly stood and thought kids could
    learn
Educators, stand firm, whether in cafeterias, mess halls,
    or prison halls,
School is in session
And we submit our entire lives for millions of students a
    year
So even when I stand in front of the class, I am always
    children first
This is not a test!
This is not a test, Ms. Rhee
This is an exam unmoved by mayoral cycles, and I?
A bubble you cannot erase
A mouth you cannot tape
A heat you cannot beat
I come in a swarm of thousands
So I am a bee you cannot eat
This is not a test!
This is not a test, Mr. President

Given an answer sheet, these students shaded in
  L-O-V-E over A-B-C-D
A set of standards commonly set forth before
Acing geography by means of peace instead of war
Shaping the world henceforth
They will elevate our math to where the sum of the
  people
Is greater than the parts
Becoming fluent in the languages of English, Spanish,
  and caring
America, please put down your pencils
This is not a test!
This is not a test!
This is not a test!
Deformers, you are dismissed.

I raised my fist and heard the cheers. The sound drowned out my weariness. I gave a half-handshake, half-hug to Pedro as I came off-stage, shaking the sweat off me, gasping for air, searching for water. I found refuge under one of the other tents, where Luz waited patiently for me. The crowd was filled with people I recognized, all thanking me for the piece. I think I fumbled through a thank-you before returning to Luz. I sat quietly under the VIP tent with her one last time before the march was officially over, letting the crowds dissipate after our march around the White House. Not one policy was proposed that day, but our common principle felt very clear. The SOS march didn't have millions of dollars or promos disguised as movies, but for the first time, it had thousands of people visibly united for a common principle.

It's a must that we bust every mic handed to us.

TO MAKE SURE IT'S BROKE
(ON TEACHER VOICE)

The spring after the Save Our Schools march, on April 28, 2012, I gave a TED talk at the Museum of the Moving Image in Queens. By then, I had gained notoriety for calling both education reformers and activists to task on a variety of issues, but my contribution had already grown from the raw to the researched in both effectiveness and incision, the difference between a butter knife and a Ginsu knife through pieces of thick steak. I could speak at an education panel in colleges and rallies alike without changing my message, just the way I said it, an important technique.

Thus, my topic was "teacher voice," a buzzword in the education field and a concept that I want to redefine because, well, I'm a teacher. I can do that. "How can we as teachers and educators in general use our voices to elevate the profession?" was the question I asked at the outset. The more I asked myself this question, the more I wanted to tackle it in a way I hadn't heard yet. I realized that we must find ways to speak up and speak out about the issues affecting our classroom and not rely on others to do that for us.

So it had to start with me.

Teachers are not given many venues to express our views on education policy, unless we are proffered to parrot the views of whomever invited us. If we're lucky, we might get to participate in a meeting with our administrators. Some of us might even get a chance to talk to our superintendents or other higher-ups, but for most of us this will be limited to "Hello" and "Thank you for your work." The communication usually flows from the top down. You'll sit there for hours on end, twiddling your thumbs, biting your lip because "Shut up!" isn't appropriate for a professional setting, going to the restroom and coming back and still not missing anything. Otherwise, teachers only get to vent our frustrations in lounges, bars, and homes. When we do have a grievance, we're either asked to take our complaints to our unions or face secretaries, locked doors, and paperwork.

I want to see the teaching profession transform to not only become less frustrating and more attuned to our ever-changing student body, but to rely on teachers in the classroom to make decisions.

And, again: I had to do it.

My decision to address teacher voice in my talk was partly inspired by the fact that one of the organizers of TEDxNYED, Basil Kolani, had told me that my poem at the Save Our Schools march had moved him to invite me to speak. In addition to feeling honored, I knew I had to speak to an idea that would be more inspirational than test scores, teacher evaluations, or Common Core. I wanted to focus on something that could serve as a resource for teachers across the world.

As research, I first asked a group of friends to define teacher voice. Their responses ranged far and wide. John Spencer, an Arizona teacher and blogger at *Education Rethink*,* said, "I'm not sure how I react." He blamed the "vilification of teachers" by corporate reformers as well as the "subtle censorship" demanded of us for robbing teachers of "agency and power and . . . our collective and individual teacher voice."

"Teachers are slow to use their voice, to speak against injustice and to recognize the power of their role in shaping paradigms and developing critical thinkers," he said.

---

* www.educationrethink.com.

This resonated with me. But then a friend, blogger John Holland, sent me this:

> Many people don't want to hear what teachers have to say. They can't hear the teacher's voice. [Educator and blogger Bill Ferriter of *The Tempered Radical**] said that policy makers refer to teachers as BMWs: bitchers, moaners, and whiners. I heard him say this in 2005. At the same time almost everyone has heard the voice of the teacher at its best: in the classroom. They may have been sucked into a story about the Revolutionary War, transported to the Supreme Court to hear a world changing debate, or gotten shivers from hearing a profound truth uttered by someone they trust. When a teacher challenges a student and the student accepts that challenge that is the teacher's voice. The teacher's voice is the challenge to reach. They have also heard the [flip side]: teachers who aren't inspired by their students or their content.
>
> Both instances are teacher voice.

As a concept, he added, teacher voice "doesn't seem concrete enough for substantive change."†

The more experienced I have become as a teacher, the more I have started to filter out people who don't bring any solutions to the table—even those whose educational ideologies match mine. It's important for teachers to come together and air our frustrations. But some people seem to love swimming in quicksand, hoping others will join them, as if the movement downward is an actual movement. I love making an irreverent joke about Arne Duncan's latest speech as much as the next activist, but after a while, my question is always, "OK, and so?" When sarcasm and vitriol are the *only* ways of discussing educational policy, we all lose. Whether face-to-face or virtual, teachers' lounges ought to feel like places for educators to recharge our batteries, not drain them out.

Being about it, any *it*, requires changing the way we talk about it, too.

---

* blog.williamferriter.com.
† John Holland, personal communication, April 7, 2012.

A few months after my talk in Queens, the city of Chicago saw a great example of the power of teacher voice when the Chicago Teachers Union (CTU) went on strike. The organizers had canvassed for years, knocking on doors, handing out information, and inspiring a new sense of hope. People of all ages and races were included in their committees and helped to elevate a teacher, Karen Lewis, to the presidency of the union. Her passion helped inspire hundreds of organizers who spoke to Chicago residents about the conditions in their public schools and the harmful effects of local, state, and federal laws on the city's children.

To wit, Jonah Edelman, CEO of the education advocacy group Stand for Children and a cabal of others, devised a law that he boasted would quell unions in Illinois. It stipulated that three panels would look into the facts of the collective bargaining agreement between the union and Chicago's board of education; if fact-finding didn't create any resolution, the union could strike. In order to call for a strike, 75 percent of the union's members would have to vote—an extremely high percentage for any union, especially a teachers' union. CTU countered with unity: almost 90 percent of its teachers supported the strike, with only 2 percent dissenting.

Xian Barrett, organizer and teacher, told me that the CTU didn't just post flyers on parents' doors. Instead, they included Chicagoans, young and elderly, in a conversation. No talking points. No "Bill Gates is evil" rhetoric. Cause and effect, in the clearest terms possible.

Malcolm X would have called this "making it plain."

As much of the media cast the teachers as striking at the expense of kids, their strike only increased the CTU's popularity and crushed the ratings of mayor and former Obama chief of staff Rahm Emanuel in the Windy City. It also served notice to the rest of the country that they ought to pay more attention to what the people at the front lines of our school system have to say. Some time later, the new schools chancellor, Barbara Byrd Bennett, shut down fifty schools permanently—the single largest wave of school closings ever in this country. At the same time, she secretly allowed charter schools to apply for space in the shuttered schools. Meanwhile, CPS administrators created "safe passages" for students dispossessed of their neighborhood schools to go to other schools miles away from their homes—passages that actually exposed them to the dangerous neighborhoods that CPS claims to want to clean up.

Mass school closings like these—which have also happened in New York, Philadelphia, and New Orleans—dilute the collective power of our teachers' unions, even as the officials behind them claim to have teachers' best interests at heart.

Some argue that leaders like Arne Duncan, Teach for America founder Wendy Kopp, or Washington, DC, schools chancellor Kaya Henderson have teachers in mind when they create policy. Others point to "teacher voice" groups like Massachusetts-based Teach Plus or New York–based Educators 4 Excellence as proof of the potential for teachers to create pockets of influence on legislation and through philanthropy. Union leaders like Randi Weingarten, president of the American Federation of Teachers, and Dennis Van Roekel, president of the National Education Association, have been lauded by many rank-and-file educators for their activism in big cities—often the epicenters for education reforms. NYU professor Diane Ravitch has captured the ears of thousands of educators across the country through her speeches and books on the deleterious effects of the No Child Left Behind and Race to the Top initiatives; Stanford professor Linda Darling-Hammond remains a voice of reason, especially in the field of educational research.

With all due respect to those I've just mentioned, rarely do I ever see an active classroom teacher in the national conversation about education. Here's something Ann Byrd, COO and partner at the Center for Teaching Quality and former National Board Certified teacher, wrote to me about teacher voice:

> When I hear "teacher voice" it reminds me of a twisted usage of synecdoche (I am grounding this in my English teaching days). "Teacher voice" suggests placing limitations on the extent to which teachers are involved—SAY things but do not DO

things. Sit at the table but do not SET the table. The powers that have called you in will HEAR you but then those powers will be the deciders and influencers, not the teachers. Teacher voice connotes a tone of "be grateful to be involved at all"— and often if teachers find themselves in a room full of people who are of this mind, if those teachers are first timers dazzled by being unleashed in public, I cringe when I hear them playing right into the script by being "so thankful" to be part of listening to the discussion. . . . Bottom line: "voice" is not nearly enough. It has to be teacher voice that communicates action and influence and decisions and impact. . . . It has to [be] LEADERSHIP. "Voice" alone is not nearly enough to be acceptable.*

Exactly.

We have to build teacher voice up to a level that commands the same respect we give doctors and lawyers. Yet, partly because this is a woman-dominated profession, teaching barely commands respect at all. In medicine and law, mostly male-dominated professions, we insist that the highest-ranking officials have years of on-the-ground experience, but our current education reform allows noneducators to make decisions on behalf of real pedagogues. Shocking.

So many of us have opinions about the way schools should run and the things society could do to help teachers. But we are sidelined and sectioned off from the billionaires and celebrities who wait in television green rooms to share their "expertise."

I almost had the nerve to redo my "This Is Not a Test" poem, but I wouldn't do that to Matt Damon. So I started to put some notes down on a slideshow, creating a collage of different things I wanted to pull in. I also started to rant on teacher voice, hoping I could pull something together in a cohesive manner. I read my old posts, hoping something would click. I even tried to see if there was a formula for perfect TED talks. Turns out there is, but I didn't use it. If I wanted different results, I would have to blow up the entire process and just flow differently.

---

* Ann Byrd, personal communication, April 7, 2012.

Like a fish swimming in the deep, dark ocean, I had to find a
way to shine from within. Bioluminescence.

As I started to jot down some notes, I saw that teacher voice
boils down to four questions:

What do you want to say?

What is your message to everyone? What do you actually want
to say? What's your point and why should it matter?

Who is your audience?

Who will be listening to what you're saying? Are you talking
to students, parents, legislators, or the general public?

How passionate are you about what you're about to say?

Do you actually believe in what you're saying? How can people tell? How much conviction do you have in what you're telling
others?

What's your solution?

Do you always start your statements with "The problem
is . . ."? If so, do you have a way to make things work or are you
just complaining? Do you see yourself as part of the change or are
you speaking to an abstract version of change?

With all disrespect, "teacher voice" doesn't mean *every* teacher's
voice, though I do want to raise every teacher's voice collectively.

So what *does* "teacher voice" mean? Ultimately I came up with
this definition: *the collective and individual expression of meaningful,
professional opinion based on classroom experience and expertise.* It makes
the most sense as a call for professionalism, autonomy, and respect
for the teaching profession. More than an argument for higher
teacher pay or better benefits, this definition opens up the potential
for teachers to ask for—even demand—a fundamental redistribution of power: from a top-down approach to one in which teachers, collectively and individually, take ownership of their roles in
reforming education, something our current set of reformers don't
all believe is necessary.

While the general public gives high trust marks to their local
teachers, many hear teacher voice as complaining rather than acting.

When people see us as complainers, we lose the chance to use our most effective teacher voice. Obviously, lots of this is gendered, too: patriarchy has a way of making women look like whiners when they voice legitimate complaints. Let's flip the image. Instead of waiting for someone to hand the mic to us, let's take it. Instead of just reiterating what others have said, let's speak from our own experiences. Instead of complaining about why teaching sucks, let's talk about why we stay.

For most of us, why we stay is the students—even the ones who don't reciprocate. The most important reason to listen to teachers is that we see our students more than anyone else does. We are their most powerful agents; we know what is in their best interests in ways that those outside the classroom do not. Anyone who claims to represent us should either come from our ranks or keep their fingers on the pulse of what teachers think and experience in schools every day.

Unions, coalitions built around whole-child ideas, and think tanks can help do this. For example, I consider people like Ravitch, Lewis, and the plethora of national experts on education who argue against edu-corporatism as powerful allies in the work we do. But in order to see them in this way, I first had to develop my own agency. I couldn't wait for a corporate sponsor, a doctoral degree, or a person from on high to validate my hard-earned experiences.

This also meant developing my own voice, which I did in part thanks to inspiration from one of my rap heroes. Rakim's legendary rhymes upped the ante on lyricism in the late eighties and early nineties with furious alliteration and ethereal metaphors. His partnership with DJ Eric B. spawned some of the best hip-hop music of all time, and that's no hyperbole. Songs like "Don't Sweat the Technique," "Follow the Leader," and "I Ain't No Joke" broke new ground by laying waste to assumptions that all raps had to follow an A-B-A-B rhyme scene. Even after decades in the rap game, rappers still borrow heavily from his works.

What always impressed me about his rhymes (and his stage performance) was the aura Rakim transmitted in his delivery. He had this supreme confidence in his performance, even while remaining humble in his interviews. Through his lyrics, he inspired hundreds of writers—not just rappers—to consider the inner workings of every line, not just the ends.

After I survived my first year of teaching, I wanted to adopt a persona that would embody the essence of how I wanted to deliver my lessons—and Rakim's style was still ripe for the stealing. In fact, when I was rehearsing my TED talk, I had his "Microphone Fiend" (1988) playing on my iPod just to help me keep my energy up.

I let this play in my head for a few weeks:

> By any means necessary, this is what has to be done
> Make way 'cause here I come
> My DJ cuts material
> Grand imperial
> It's a must that I bust any mic you hand to me,
> It's inherited, it runs in the family
> I wrote the rhyme that broke the bull's back,
> If that don't slow 'em up, I carry a full pack.*

When the big day came for the TED talk, I was already bopping my head backstage to these few lines. Sweating bullets in my red sweater, I started enunciating too. I was still shocked at myself that I had included one of Rakim's raps in the actual talk, something I don't believe had been done in any TEDx presentations.

With that much power, you'd think he wouldn't *need* to get better at rhyming, but he does. I incorporated 1992's "Don't Sweat The Technique" into my speech too:

> They wanna know how many rhymes have I ripped in
>   rep, but
> Researchers never found all the pieces yet

---

* Eric B. & Rakim, "Microphone Fiend," *Follow the Leader*, UNI Records, 1988.

Scientists try to solve the context
Philosophers are wondering what's next
Pieces are took to last who observe them
They couldn't absorb them, they didn't deserve them
My ideas are only for the audience's ears
For my opponents, it might take years
Pencils and pens are swords
Letters put together form a key to chords
I'm also a sculpture, born with structure
Because of my culture, I'mma rip and destruct the
Difficult styles that'll be for the technology
Complete sights and new heights after I get deep
You don't have to speak, just seek
And peep the technique.*

Rakim exemplifies the power of developing an authentic voice, one that reflects your own experiences. He sounds like excellence, achieved through hardship and strife. Everything from his gravelly, booming speech to his message of knowledge, peace, and understanding comes in crystal clear. Rakim came to command the universal respect of any rapper with a modicum of influence on hip-hop culture.

In the same way, I started to see that developing a teacher voice required three cogent pieces: a balance between emotion and reason; expert confidence; and a specific audience in mind. Often, the audience is not our students. One place that can be a venue for teacher voice is our teachers' lounge. This can be good or bad. Teachers' lounges serve as breathing spaces, not just places to eat lunch, make photocopies, or grade homework. If, in the company of colleagues, we happen to discuss our frustrations, that's healthy—to a point. If anything, teachers' lounges matter in terms of convenience and sanity.

---

* Eric B. & Rakim, "Don't Sweat the Technique," *Don't Sweat the Technique*, MCA Records, 1992.

Yet if we sit too long in the lounge, a few things tend to occur. The place can stun—if not stomp on—any momentum you've built for your teaching. Sometimes, two or three teachers with a soapbox (but no plan for direct or indirect action) will hold court for the benefit of both willing and unwilling audience members. Sometimes the arguments get heated, much to the chagrin of those just trying to eat lunch—and to the pleasure of anyone who might be secretly feeding names and accusations to the principal or other administration members. Gossip abounds, sapping the energy teachers would otherwise reserve for their next class.

In my third year of teaching, instead of getting jaded, I got active.

I developed my own blog, created my stalwart persona on social media, and joined the Center for Teaching Quality (CTQ).

As I mentioned a few chapters back, I first found out CTQ through my friend John Holland, who found me through other people's links to my blog. By then I had developed a small platform and a community of commenters willing to engage me in discussions about the classroom. At the heart of CTQ was the Teacher Leaders Network, a virtual platform moderated by editor and Middleweb founder John Norton, where I found dozens of open-minded and solutions-focused teachers who shared their deepest hardships, greatest triumphs, and general inquiries, a stark contrast from the teachers' lounge conversations that drain so many of us. That community helped elevate the policy voice that I use to this day.

In 2010, I got a phone call from Arthur Wise, school-finance reform advocate and chairman of CTQ's board of directors. At first I thought I had said something to get the organization into trouble, but in fact he wanted me to join the board, sitting alongside him as well as the likes of American Association of Colleges of Teacher Education president Sharon Robinson and National Board for Professional Teaching Standards founder James Kelly. Saying yes made me only the second teacher to have served on the board at the time. I took on the role so that I could listen to what CTQ wanted to accomplish and see if it connected to how the teachers in my real and virtual communities felt. I joined. Sitting on the board with such major figures made me apprehensive at first, but once I saw the value of my teacher voice and the purpose for my presence on the board, I came to see them as colleagues.

Shut up, José, you belong here.

♦

I don't see myself as the *only* one who has this voice. In fact, I stand on the shoulders of giants, and I met many of them through CTQ. Nationally acclaimed educator Renee Moore was the first educator of color I met who spoke about her teaching as rooted in the histories of Black people across generations, not as a solitary act of kindness. She often engages people to rethink the role of race and gender in education and she has a knack for candor that draws people into her audience. In 2011 she was invited to participate on a panel on the reauthorization of the Elementary and Secondary Education Act—otherwise known as No Child Left Behind (NCLB). She used her allotted time to chastise local and federal government officials for their misguided emphasis on standardized testing and school funding proposals. She excoriated almost every public policy official present, as well as those back in her home state of Mississippi.

> Though it has some good intentions, because NCLB was so poorly conceived, and poorly implemented, it has been used to dilute curriculum, manacle teachers, and humiliate students, exactly the opposite of what it takes to improve education. Much of this collateral damage could have been avoided had it not gone down the path of distrusting teachers and settling uncritically for quick and dirty ways of measuring student learning and teachers' worth.[*]

---

[*] Renee Moore, shown in a video posted by YouTube user "vangogh111," "ESEA Reauthorization Panel - Renee Moore Rocks the Boat," delivered at the ESEA Reauthorization Panel in San Diego on February 24, 2011, posted February 28, 2011, www.youtube.com/watch?v=Pbo9RZJno0M.

Her voice alone makes her speech worth a listen on YouTube, but her audience, a room full of education policy makers and theorists, must have been shocked—SHOCKED—that a teacher could so passionately and deftly strip down their arguments. Then again, such a surprise might be the reason why we're not invited into those inner circles. If teachers had any business in those meetings on a substantial level, many of the suits and ties in the room would have to vacate their seats for us. The largest threat to any set of education reforms is a well-informed and vocal set of teachers, parents, and students.

After all, teachers had known for a decade that No Child Left Behind wouldn't work. Can we afford another decade to realize Race to the Top won't work either?

Thus, I tied all my thoughts together with a pretty bow and called my TED talk "Redefining Teacher Voice." It was a full fifteen minutes of me talking uninterrupted. Let me tell you: in class, that never happens. After my fifteen minutes were up, I hoped my message would resonate with so many who want a new vision for educators, a redefinition for those who can't quite pinpoint what makes their jobs so critical. Even with my scientific approach, I don't think developing your voice takes much more than plenty of practice and an ability to listen more than you bloviate.

As resistance to our current set of reforms strengthens, "teacher voice" becomes even more important.

Even when toiling against these education-reform trends—or the challenges of teaching in general—leads to despair or cynicism, a teacher's voice can still create something positive. Teachers must develop a tough exterior—not just to withstand our students' temperaments, but also to support each other as we navigate the political and economic whims of those who set the policies that affect us most. Until then, we have to strengthen our voices, speak from our experiences and those of our students, assume and defend our autonomy, and kick butt at every turn.

GETTING LESS THAN YOU GIVE
(ON COMMON CORE STATE STANDARDS)

[The two most popular forms of writing are] the exposition of a personal opinion [and] the presentation of a personal narrative. The only problem, forgive me for saying this so bluntly, the only problem with those two forms of writing is that, as you grow up in this world, you come to realize that *no one really gives a shit about what you feel or what you think.*

This is what David Coleman, architect of the Common Core State Standards and president of the College Board (which creates the SATs), told a captive audience at the New York State Department of Education during an April conference in 2011. Coleman's salvo lit a fuse in an already heated debate about what kids ought to learn in school.

As I watched via simulcast, I let out an emphatic "Huh."

By the time I entered education in 2005, No Child Left Behind—a partisan policy meant to appease the left's need for a focus on the lowest-performing schools with the right's need for accountability and data—was in its fourth year. Teachers, schools, and districts had already amassed thousands of "data points" (read: students) to track for compliance with an obscure set of regulations in order to unlock different types of school funding. Mayor Bloomberg had already spent millions of dollars on bulky data storage systems and droves of young, inexperienced staff to bulk up accountability task forces.

183

Newbies like me had never known a school system without standards, objectives, or pacing calendars. We were asked to follow the curriculum to the best of our abilities, to use the textbooks we were given, and to not make too much fuss about it. Veterans of the system would whisper that NCLB took the joy out of teaching while pleasing the datamaniacs with binders full of printed Excel spreadsheets, sample assessments, and reports. While the gains from NCLB aren't clear to the everyday teacher, the effects on our school system are—and they work visibly to our detriment.

People who spend far too much time thinking about education research (including yours truly) tend to fall in one of two camps. The first is the constructivists, who believe in learning through exploration, like famed Italian educator Maria Montessori and one of the fathers of modern education, John Dewey. The other is the behaviorists, who favor learning through rigid, experimental methods, like psychologist and educator Edward Thorndike. While the first group gets more attention, the second group has enjoyed a resurgence in the past thirteen years with the renewed attention being given to standards, data, and testing (in that order).

The current iteration of the standards movement was born in the 1980s, when a group of concerned intellectuals came together and charted everything they thought a teenager should know by the time he or she gets a high-school diploma. Key among them was David Pierpont Gardner, who chaired a special commission in 1983 under the authority of Secretary of Education T. H. Bell. Its report, *A Nation at Risk*, was an alarmist response to concerns that the United States was lagging behind other industrialized nations. Among its many recommendations, which included structured requirements for high-school students and professionally competitive salaries for teachers, the published report called for a focus on what we teach children:

> Our goal must be to develop the talents of all to their fullest. Attaining that goal requires that we expect and assist all students to work to the limits of their capabilities. We should expect

schools to have genuinely high standards rather than minimum
ones, and parents to support and encourage their children to
make the most of their talents and abilities.*

By the time the first George Bush came around in the late 1980s,
legislators were ready to set educational goals for the year 2000 aimed
at a uniform, state-by-state understanding of the country's educational mission for every child, regardless of sex, race, class, or background. Numerous political battles ensued, but the Bush and Clinton
administrations kept the idea of "outcomes-based education" afloat
until George W. Bush made it official with the signing of the No
Child Left Behind Act of 2001. The law ushered in an era of escalat-
ing accountability measures. Schools were asked to identify their lowest performers in specific categories and to take steps to raise their
academic performance. Schools that failed to achieve an acceptable
average for test scores were threatened with being shut down.

This trend was only exacerbated by the Obama administration's Race to the Top program, unveiled in 2009, which has states
compete for federal funding by demonstrating a plan to improve
teaching and learning, measured mainly through test scores. States
spent months compiling reports to detail how they would spend
such money on more accountability measures and evaluation systems, as well as on ways to break existing caps on the number of
charter schools allowed in their respective school systems.

In the same year, a bipartisan group of governors called the
Council of Chief State School Officers came together to reach an
agreement on setting uniform standards for their states. Student
Achievement Partners, David Coleman's group, then concretized
what we have come to know as the Common Core State Standards
(CCSS). Politically, adopting such standards was a win for both
sides. Democrats could announce that it had taken a step toward

---

* National Commission on Excellence in Education, *A Nation at Risk: The Imperative for Educational Reform* (Washington, DC: Department of Education, 1983),
http://datacenter.spps.org/uploads/SOTW_A_Nation_at_Risk_1983.pdf.

equity by making sure children in every classroom across the country would receive the same instruction. Republicans could proclaim that these standards set benchmarks for competition against the world's top-performing countries, ensuring that the United States would retain its dominance.

With business leaders, unions, and professors from across the nation engaged in this work, everyone involved got to say they had a voice in how they came together. Business leaders liked the aspect of contributing to the K–12 education system with the intention of creating a capable workforce for the twenty-first century. Unions could point to equity and the need to define expectations more clearly throughout the country, not just in specific locales. Even today, our national unions—and teachers in their ranks—hope that teachers can and will take the lead on implementing the standards, showing the general public that, yes, they want to cooperate rather than obstruct these seemingly thoughtful ideas. Professors could claim some credit and hoped that the standards would mean a decrease in the need for remedial classes at the college level, since more students would be able to write well enough for regular coursework. And, using a loophole in constitutional law, states could adopt the standards in exchange for a chance at Race to the Top money.

Indeed, from the outside, the Common Core seems to be good for all involved. In times of austerity, switching from state standards (or, in many cases, no standards) for a set of internationally benchmarked, researched, vetted, and well-funded standards is a no-brainer. All's well that ends well. Except, that is, for those the Common Core's proponents neglected to consider: students, teachers, and parents.

The fact that the initial list of CCSS's creators, which is full of presidents of organizations and professors of one thing and another, doesn't include a *single* student or teacher speaks volumes about our current approach to education.* With all due respect to the

---

* Thanks, Anthony Cody. National Governors Association, "Common Core State Standards Development Work Group and Feedback Group Announced," July 1, 2009, http://bit.ly/1pyFSkn.

presidents and professors I know, lists like this don't usually bode well for teacher voice. After some pushback from teachers' unions and other concerned individuals, a couple of classroom teachers were added to the feedback groups, but, from what I've seen, their opinions were probably met with an "OK, thank you, we'll take that into consideration while we do what we want anyway."

Just about everyone gets a seat at the proverbial table to design the curriculum—except the people executing that curriculum. Americans would not expect to see a military general without experience in the field or a head surgeon who's never operated on anyone. Yet we trust people with no classroom experience to tell us what and how our students should learn.

Part of the problem is that people can now make the case that most teachers do not have enough experience to design curricula. So many teachers now come to the profession via alternative certification programs that the average teacher's years of experience have dwindled. When it comes to our most vulnerable students, we've turned teaching into a domestic Peace Corps. No disrespect to the Peace Corps, but the fact is that for our first year of teaching, most of us are just trying to survive. The students with the greatest needs ought to have the most experienced and best-equipped teachers, ideally teachers who are open to new methods but who also have their own set of strategies for reaching students.

When I was a rookie, I succeeded because my school had veteran teachers of all ages. Without this kind of mix, it's hard to create a learning community for both children and adults. New teachers bring idealism and energy. Veteran teachers bring wisdom and pedagogical knowledge. None of it matters if they can't coalesce around a common experience.

As far as I'm concerned, standards are training wheels, a baseline teachers can use to build a set of goals. Over time, teachers will assess the effectiveness of the activities they have designed and use "teachable moments" to their advantage when things don't go according to plan.

But the CCSS has allowed publishers to insinuate themselves deeper still into teachers' curricula. They slap "Common Core aligned" stickers on their products regardless of whether those products are actually aligned with the standards. They provide online materials that contain glitches and are confusing to navigate in the hopes that teachers stay on their pages as long as possible. Then they can turn around to the districts, show their page-view statistics, and say, "See, teachers are just not adjusting well to the new technologies. Give us more money to help us fix this." If a teacher still doesn't get it, textbook publishing companies like Pearson are happy to dispatch instructional coaches to come in and provide "professional development" on the product (not to mention criticism of anyone who dares to question its value). If a teacher still can't be convinced, an assistant principal or coach might whisper a few things to the principal about said dissident being "out of compliance."

Any initiative, even one as intriguing as the CCSS, sows seeds of distrust as long as the structures of our school system stay in place.

Because of its rushed and compulsory implementation, the CCSS looks less like an instructional shift and more like a money-making operation. The billions now spinning through public education to pay for third-party professional development, curriculum materials, speakers, and technology should make everyone skeptical. We have CCSS apps on our smartphones to help us identify which standard belongs with which grade and CCSS T-shirts to help others identify who's been trained in the Common Core. We have CCSS fellowships to identify people who've mastered a set of standards that only came out a few years ago and big education-focused foundations that force grantees large and small to turn their efforts toward Common Core—because this is what we do now.

We have TV programs telling the country that teachers are trying their best to adhere to the Common Core State Standards, which is code for "trying really hard to teach really hard." The commercial breaks feature Sal Khan's Khan Academy, a library of free videos funded primarily by the Gates Foundation that serves as a next-generation lecture device. Instead of having a teacher stand in front of thirty students to explain a topic in person, students can pull up a video of Khan teaching the lesson and replay it as often as they like. That way, teachers don't have to stand in front of the classroom lecturing and can instead focus on doing classroom activities and differentiating for every student.

This sounds great until you realize the major flaw in Khan's logic. Now, instead of individual teachers who can adjust their lesson plans to the needs of the class, you have a million students receiving the same exact lesson from someone who has no idea whom he's teaching.* Yet, because the glossy commercials full of fuzzy feelings run like memes across a Facebook timeline, people believe it with little understanding of Khan Academy's implications for a generation of students in need of an expert teacher who sees them for *who* they are (as people) as much as *what* they are (as students).

We also have CCSS tests to tell states and the children who don't pass that they're failures. These kids must either get tutoring or stay after school. Their teachers, who just learned these standards themselves, are considered to have failed them, too. And then the schools are said to have failed—so they *must* be shut down, in the name of accountability, and turned over to someone else.

All of this based on tests whose cutoff scores are determined arbitrarily and on the fly for political reasons.

I don't believe that everyone who agrees with the CCSS is a shill for corporate education, just as I don't think everyone who hates the CCSS still wants to teach kids multiplication tables in eighth grade. Teaching multiplication tables is fine for a period of remediation but would work better if integrated into lessons about linear relationships and scientific notation, not as a standalone unit study of

---

*And some would argue he doesn't always know *what* he's teaching. Robert Talbert, "The Trouble with Khan Academy," *Casting Our Nines,* July 3, 2012, http://chronicle.com/blognetwork/castingoutnines/2012/07/03/the-trouble-with-khan-academy.

lessons. Plenty of people who like the Common Core, including business leaders and think-tank presidents, believe in teacher voice, strong professional development, and better learning conditions for teachers and students. Despite what we might read, most teachers I know just want to make it work despite a lack of resources, time, or understanding. They're getting paid to do a job and the CCSS has become a part of that responsibility. That includes yours truly.

I just believe every initiative we undertake should be scrutinized and carefully rolled out without immediately demanding account-ability from those who are charged with executing it. As Diana Laufenberg says, we can have standards without standardization:

> The reason that the Common Core is so hard for me to talk about is that I believe it is the WRONG conversation. It assumes that the "what" of teaching and learning was inadequate, which has then led to American mediocrity. And now that the stan-dards are common ... if we can juuuuust standardize the "how," all of education's ills will be "solved." No static list of learning objectives coupled with standardized methods is going to EVER get us moving in the direction we need to be moving. . . .
> I can tolerate that there are common standards, but I can't seem to tolerate that it then tacitly means that the art of my craft needs to be standardized, boiled down to mediocrity, so as to guarantee outcomes.*

But you didn't ask her. Or me. So we're not completely buying the "college- and career-ready" crap.

I'm not just coming from left field. As someone who's delved into the Common Core for four years, I've read the CCSS stan-dards in math and literacy backward and forward, working within the lingo and getting a grasp of the differences between our old New York State Standards and the new Common Core State Stan-dards. It might not seem like a major difference, but in many ways

---

* Diana Laufenberg, "Standards, Not Standardization," *Living the Dream*, December 27, 2013, http://laufenberg.wordpress.com/2013/12/27 /standards-not-standardization.

it's pushed me to teach my eighth-graders more advanced math. While CCSS advocates boast that these standards lighten the amount of work teachers have to do, depth has replaced breadth. I may not teach as many topics, but I most definitely teach as much if not more with these standards, running up to the very last topic one week before the "big test."

Studies show that people in other countries don't worry about covering the entire curriculum and still get high scores, but I always wonder if teachers in other countries get held to the same ridiculous accountability systems, with the same resources and the same discourse about "bad teachers." Every day, when I'm planning lessons and activities, prompting discussion, pushing students to get engaged, I wonder if it wouldn't be more efficient just to teach directly to the test without the added effort of making them self-sufficient learners, free from the responsibility of having to think about the work in front of them.

Must be nice.

But if you asked me, I'd do things a bit differently.

In New York, for instance, I would have asked that all teacher data reports be tossed out the window. Ostensibly, these reports rank teachers based on students' gains in English Language Arts and math over a given time period. But there are a few problems here. In February 2012, after the NYC Department of Education promised it wouldn't release the already-controversial teacher data reports to the general public (as several media organizations had requested), they somehow leaked anyway and every major newspaper in New York City released them for all the world to see. When I searched for my own, I learned a few facts about myself that the general public could easily misinterpret. According to the reports, in the 2009–2010 school year, I ranked in the seventh percentile—with a margin of error of 25 percent. In the 2012–13 school year, I earned a score of 39 percent—with a margin of error of *41 percent.*

Taken at face value, this would make it seem like, with me as their teacher, my students only had a 39 percent chance of moving to higher proficiency on their math exams. But this is deeply misleading. The astonishingly high margin of error of 41 percent means that my score could have swerved into the sixty-first percentile or the twenty-first percentile, but this report was *absolutely sure* I was at the thirty-ninth percentile. According to one study, after five years the margin of error comes down to a 30 percent average, which falls to 11 percent in a teacher's tenth year.* In other words, by the time these scores even get close to predicting how my students will do on tests, we have a much better measure of their performance because they are old enough to have graduated from college. There's also a good chance that the teacher might not have stayed a teacher long enough for any of this to actually matter.

It quickly reminded me of the financial market crash of 2008, where Wall Street had spent much of the country's collective fortunes on the hopes that a formula developed by a leading economist with invalid assumptions would keep the profits coming. As is always the case, the most damage based on these risks lands on the heads of the 99.9 percent of us who didn't know this equation existed to begin with.

When I first wrote about this, my email and phone immediately blew up with media requests. Perhaps reporters saw a teacher willing to speak openly and convincingly about his own data report, flaws and all. When my local FOX affiliate contacted me, the reporter first searched through my blog for any sort of incriminating evidence ("Is that a picture of Snoop Dogg smoking weed? What is that there?"), then wondered if I was free for an interview on their morning show. I scoffed at myself for even considering the opportunity. Then I laughed at the irony of speaking up in an interview about putting students first when taking on the interview would make me late for class. (Needless to say, I didn't do it, but the interviews and writing opportunities I did take made a

---

* Richard Rothstein et al., "Problems with the Use of Student Test Scores to Evaluate Teachers," Economic Policy Institute briefing paper, August 27, 2010, www.epi.org/publications/entry/bp278.

dent—and perhaps made me some quiet enemies. Welp.)

If it were up to me, I would have waited to impose the CCSS-based accountability measures and to publicize schools' scores. Teachers and schools need time to adjust to such standards. I would work to keep expert teachers in the schools and have them run the professional development around curriculum. This would create real teacher leadership that would probably help everyone involved, especially students. Having the professors who developed the CCSS come down from on high to tell us how much time we should spend on each standard, without an understanding of how long each standard actually takes to teach, doesn't help in the least if those professors don't work with us. From there, I would take inventory in schools to figure out who has what expertise and use them across the district to provide models of how to approach pedagogy in different content areas.

Even as I write this, the New York State Board of Regents, our state's governing education body, has "listened to parents and educators" and recommended that the state postpone accountability measures for five years, resuming their agenda in 2019 or 2020. At a cursory glance, one might think Board of Regents chancellor Merryl Tisch spearheaded these changes out of the goodness of her heart. To the contrary, it was the vociferous protests of parents, students, and educators in concert working in those community board meetings that assured the people's voice was heard. Civility only works when the more powerful side is willing to relinquish power—and with so many politicians uncritically taking on reforms, the collective grassroots has to take on whole-child advocacy from different sides.

None of this means that teachers in the classroom aren't doing their jobs. If anything, we know we have to work harder, better, and smarter. Many of the teachers protesting these reforms happen to have excellent test scores and phenomenal recommendations from their principals. Like the university scholars who protest the SATs and ACTs, even those who benefit from our accountability system take issue with getting measured solely on the merits of an outside, decontextualized, monied source.

That's why so many of us feel like we're getting less than what we give. Deteriorating working conditions make it harder for teachers to stay in the classroom; those of us who do work harder just to make up for the deficit. We give more and more, but it often feels like we get less respect, less funding, less attention, less of a stake in the way schools should run. This may or may not have been caused by the CCSS, but one thing is clear: the standards are but a symptom of a system that devalues the input of the very people it affects.

I would have asked teachers like me all along, during every step of the process. But they didn't ask us because teachers like me have an opinion—and we all know how David Coleman feels about opinions.

THE EAGLE VERSUS
THE HUMMINGBIRD:
A CAUTIONARY NOTE TO BURGEONING
TEACHER LEADERS

Dear burgeoning teacher leader,

Congratulations. You've been chosen/selected/promoted to a position of leadership in your school. Whether you're an instructional coach, an assistant principal, or a lead teacher, your achievements up to this point merit applause. I hope that the benefits and challenges of the position you're about to undertake have been outlined for you. If not, rest assured that it will be hard as hell. But someone needed you somewhere and so I suppose they saw something in you.

If you're coming from the classroom, though, I should caution you: you're trading intimacy in for effect.

This is where I tell you to run away from such titles. Scurry, not shuffle, your feet back to the classroom. It's not that simple.

When people talk to me about the possibility of becoming an administrator, they say that I could be taking my talents to higher ground, that instead of reaching thirty to ninety students I could reach three hundred, five hundred, even eight hundred at a time. This might be true, but the real value would be in finding a balance between improving teaching quality at a given school and actually getting to know the students it would affect.

When people first found out that I had been promoted to math coach in June 2009, the reactions ranged from caution ("You really want to do this?") to jealousy ("Him?") to pride ("YEAH BOY!") and elation ("Oh word?"). A math coach is an instructional leader for the building who helps teachers with their pedagogy in whatever capacity he or she can. An instructional coach also takes on different responsibilities, including working with students one-on-one or sometimes co-teaching to help another teacher out. I begged to take on at least one class, which gave me buy-in with all the other math teachers, all of whom had more years of experience than I did at the time.

A few people whispered that I was too young and inexperienced for the position. Others said it was about time someone with a more empathetic voice took charge of the math department. Either way, I didn't come into the position with a superiority complex but with a strong desire to make changes that would benefit the entire department—but some quickly and wrongly dismissed me as a principal's favorite. I intended to be the best possible liaison between the administration, teachers, and students. I didn't quite know what that would look like just then, but I wanted a shot at it. Instead I found myself stuck in a single dimension of the job: the out-of-classroom time.

My fiancée would call that the difference between intention and effect.

Fortunately, I had a mentor, Mr. Fishkin, who had been the math consultant and coach just before me. He let me bounce ideas off him, and we shared similar frustrations about the job as a whole. He got me through some of my difficult moments (see "Yes, I Still Want To Teach"). Learning how to work with individual teachers, analyze state exams and deliver those results to teachers, and make assessments more challenging were just some of the things I learned from him. I still imagine him picking up Sudoku puzzles and sifting through the *New York Times* for math articles in his retirement getaway.

I also relished the times I could just sit in a classroom and help students out during their classwork periods. And I appreciated the colleagues who (eventually) saw me supporting rather than evaluating them when I walked into their classrooms.

Balancing my practice as coach and teacher made my head spin. In my first year of coaching, I missed about three weeks' worth of instructional time due to professional development sessions, district-level meetings, and more. I might teach in the morning but find myself in the middle of a brainstorming session in the afternoon. I ran around the school putting out fires and fixing calculators and projects. I welcomed the opportunity to help teachers resolve issues with their immediate supervisors, but often hoped they would find the power in themselves to integrate the administrator's feedback into their style. My overtime (what NYC DOE calls "per-session" time) was usually spent trying to clean up after myself, decompressing from an exhausting day with children and adults. It was difficult keeping up with learning how to be a math coach to more than eight hundred students while also ensuring that all of my assigned eighth-graders got what they needed from me.

In my first year as math coach, my students and I didn't do as well as we could have academically. My relationship with them didn't necessarily suffer, but neither did it help to be consistently absent for random reasons. In my second year, I handled my responsibilities much better. I worked harder to keep up with my class's academic needs. I visited classrooms more often. I delved deeper into curriculum and pedagogy. I even dealt with some disciplinary and administrative matters. Yet because of the energy needed to do all that, I didn't devote as much of my emotional energy to the students in my classroom—and it showed. I didn't want to be distant, but there's only so much energy human beings have.

When you're strictly a classroom teacher, you can just worry about your own students. When things go wrong, it's easy to say that it's the leader's fault, whoever that leader is. If you're an instructional coach, you hope the moral and pedagogical support you provide boosts achievement for students and teachers. If you're a curriculum developer, you hope the materials you've laid out and the curriculum plans you've developed boost achievement. If you're a dean or a coordinator for a floor, unofficially an administrator, you're hoping the floor runs smoothly, with as little disruption as possible in and out of classrooms, so children can learn, which then boosts achievement. When you're a teacher leader or any sort of leader, you're not just worried about the brains learning, but also the brains teaching and the brains working to support those who are teaching and learning, all simultaneously.

My changed perception as a math coach had a domino effect on how I viewed principals, superintendents, and everyone at the central offices. They make tough decisions quietly on a daily basis.

In many education leadership trainings, people like to compare leadership styles to animals. So I propose we think about the difference between a teacher and a teacher leader as the difference between a hummingbird and an eagle. From a distance, the hummingbird has less presence than an eagle—but look again. A hummingbird's tools allow it to taste the sweet with the sour more precisely and with more intimacy. Eagles, by contrast, cover more ground due to their size and flight. They don't get as close to the ground; they can see from a large distance away. The price for being at the top of the food chain is that they're exposed to more chemicals, making their position equally perilous. Once you trade in the classroom key for a master key to the entire school, people marvel at how you've learned to soar. But humans, unlike eagles, have a choice and ought to determine for themselves how wide to spread their wings.

As for me, I was slowly phased out of the math coaching position for reasons I still can't pinpoint. New York City educator and friend Stephen Lazar says teacher leaders shouldn't stay more than three years in one position and, indeed, my time ran out. I didn't like letting go but respected the decision. More importantly, with all the opportunities I had been granted through the Center for Teaching Quality and through writing for the *Huffington Post* and *Edutopia*, I didn't just see the writing on the wall: I had written it. I was going from acting as an instructional leader in the building to acting as one of the more unique voices in the education sphere, and I hadn't expected it. By the time administration moved me to my current role as a student advocate, I was already feeling the tug to do more as a teacher leader across the whole system, to act as a self-appointed edu–life coach; working as a student advocate allowed me to speak up and out at will.

Even as I tuck in and go back to the classroom full-time, my sharp eyes and large wingspan let me fly.

Signed,

The Eagle

EVERY DAY ABOVE GROUND
IS A GOOD ONE

"Nah, I don't feel like it, nigga. Leave me alone!"

The day began like any other during my tenure as math coach. I hopped into the library first thing in the morning, grabbed my book cart, whisked it into my assigned room for the day, and started setting up as the students walked in. By the time the bell rang at eight o'clock, I was ready with iPad in hand, taking attendance. The bulk of the students arrived by 8:02, enough time for me to get my objective and "Do Now" activity on the SMART Board that I'd turned into a whiteboard because my school laptop takes twenty minutes to load up. Pencils scratched notebooks as I prompted my students to think about the activity, a segue into my lesson for the day. I sighed loudly at the few students who came in at 8:15, but continued the lesson to honor those who had arrived on time.

At around 8:25, well into my lesson, JJ, the "bad kid," walked into the classroom.

I said "Good morning." He didn't reciprocate. He sat in the back of the classroom. I asked him to get up and go to his assigned seat. He said no. I prompted him to do it again. He obliged, dragging his feet. Everyone stared. I waved my hands in a circular motion, trying to get the rest of the class back to work. JJ pulled out his binder. I smirked a bit. He started writing something. I smirked a bit more. I walked around to see others working on their assignments. JJ had his head down in his notebook.

I looked over his shoulder. He was working on an assignment for a different class. I shook my head in disapproval.

"JJ, I need you to get back to work on the assignment we have today."

"No."

"JJ, I *need* you to try this. It's not too difficult. I need *something* from you, anything at all."

"No!"

"OK, let's try this again. You're in my math class. We already spoke about the work you need to get done in my class. This is how you succeed in my class."

"Nah, I don't feel like it, nigga. Leave me alone!"

I cocked my head back, surprised at the way he had addressed me. I walked away for a second, then asked him to step out. He took his stuff and made his way to his usual chair in the dean's office. I continued with my lesson, hoping I hadn't come off as too rattled in front of the other students. After class, I peeked inside the dean's office and found JJ gone, perhaps for the rest of the day. I walked into my station in the principal's office and stared at the computer screen.

Before that moment I had written long notes to JJ, hoping he would read them and feel inspired to give himself a shot. Every so often, he actually *wanted* to be in class. As the "bad kid" he walked the hallways when he chose, pushed boys and girls in and out of the classroom, never wore a uniform, told teachers off, and cut out of eighth period. He became well acquainted with the deans and assistant principals. Like so many others who get this label, also served as a foil, an example adults could point to and say, "Don't be like him!"

One person who never bought into the "bad kid" stereotype was Ms. Elana Waldman.

This aggressive, red-haired Jewish woman with her sturdy walk always strolled into a room with an exasperated face—or an "I need a smoke" face; they were hard to differentiate. Her shouts shook her classroom walls so much that even the adults didn't venture near her classroom. My first interaction with Ms. Waldman wasn't at a faculty meeting or in the teachers' lounge. It was about six feet from her classroom, where she almost blew the door off with her bellow.

I had heard about her reputation for her classroom management and work ethic. In more ways than one. But it was her boundless dedication to the "bad kids," the ones who had little faith in their own academic abilities, that made an impression on me. She knew she could shout over them, but that didn't satisfy her. She spent plenty of time getting in their faces about work but also tried to understand them on a personal level. This rabbi's daughter turned bookie and pool shark, who told us stories of dirty pool halls and the miscreants who roamed them, found an unlikely home teaching impoverished Black and Latino kids in Washington Heights. Luz and Zuleika—my friend and social-studies counterpart in my first year—had brought her under their wings when she arrived, but she had grown into her own by the time I befriended her.

She loved telling the story of Jason, a kid with whom she had stayed in touch, writing letters and driving up to prison to give him moral support. Jason had had a reputation since the first day he walked the halls for misbehaviors. I never interacted with him personally, but I had heard other teachers' stories. Some were happy not to have him, but Ms. Waldman would always smile when recounting Jason and the other knuckleheads and rambunctious kids. She identified with them. Jason was perhaps the first kid who made her realize this, and she had kept mental note of all her "bad" kids ever since.

It was not until 2011 that I finally got a chance to be her math counterpart in class 814. Half the class was made up of students with regular programs; the other half had individualized education programs, which required an integrated co-teacher along with the subject teacher in the room. The class was a microcosm of the school as a whole. The valedictorian-level nerds hung out with the yearbook and stage-crew kids. My Penny Harvest kids* pretended to be gangsta and argued over the relative greatness of Kobe Bryant, LeBron James, and Kevin Durant. One of the girls ostracized herself with a bad attitude toward everyone but her teachers. JJ, on the other hand, found a way to weave in and out of all the groups, using his wit to disarm even those who felt a little intimidated by his aggressive behavior.

As I taught alongside Ms. Waldman throughout the first semester, we had our ups and downs. My book cart clashed with her classroom aesthetic; her views on race clashed with my pride. I'd post something on Facebook about how some current event gave us a lens as to how far our country has to go on race relations and she would reply, "That's not true! Oh, that's just like what my kids would say when I tell them they can't go to the bathroom. 'That's racist, miss!' *No it isn't!* Not everything is racism!" *Oy vey.*

At times it felt great tag-teaming with such a solid and candid English teacher. Other times, I dismissed her ideas because they killed my vibe. But she was always putting the kids above her ego; she did that so well.

Later that year, however, Ms. Waldman delivered devastating news to our school: she was slowly losing her battle with cancer. Over the next four years, her health and appearance fluctuated. We hoped that the chemo and tumor removals would vanquish this amorphous venom from her body, but they never did.

Even as she was in treatment, though, Ms. Waldman focused on brainstorming how we might engage JJ. Nothing we tried seemed to work. We couldn't bring him in before school because he had a hard time just getting to school on time, let alone early. We couldn't bring him in after school because he already disappeared before eighth period came around. During school, we had

---

* Penny Harvest is a nonprofit dedicated to teaching children philanthropy and community service through collecting pennies in schools. Schools usually organize student leadership teams to administer the Penny Harvest program. You can learn more at www.commoncents.org/go/penny-harvest/about-the-penny-harvest.

twenty-eight other students who needed our attention, half of whom would not work if we left them to their own devices.

Besides, JJ found himself in a bit of trouble at every turn: fights outside school, bullying students in class, disputes with both his adoptive and biological mothers, drug possession charges that prompted visits from parole officers. When he was in class, he slept. When he wasn't in class, it was easier to teach but we felt uneasy. We hoped he was safe.

That year I came up with my 10 percent theory. No matter how hard I tried, how much I yelled or didn't, how long I stayed after school working on differentiated assessments, or how many books I read on child development, I found that I couldn't reach about 10 percent of my students. For every thirty students, I knew that ten of them would succeed no matter who stood in front of them because of their effort, their intelligence, or both. A critical seventeen of the students could turn the whole class, either doing well if the teacher kept up with them or poorly if the teacher wasn't prepared. This left three or four students who simply didn't break through. For any number of reasons, I simply couldn't make the magic happen with them; they eventually would fall through the cracks. I blamed myself more than anything else. Even as my mentors assured me, "If you even reach one student every day, you're doing a good job," my stubborn self couldn't accept that. I wanted all my students to succeed in some capacity and got up every morning with every intention of investing in these students.

Yet I couldn't break through. I would have loved to point the finger at poverty, family issues, the lack of structure or routine in their lives, or the lack of a consistent support system that might have helped alleviate their angst. I just couldn't. I can only blame the things I can control: me. Perhaps Ms. Waldman perhaps blamed herself too. She and I shared a passion for children that didn't allow us to give up. However, unlike me, Ms. Waldman had a larger threshold for the behaviors of the "bad" ones. She wanted to know their stories, delve into their lives, and empathize in ways that she couldn't with the nerds, geeks, and nice kids. Like me.

That's why, when I first started the school year, I thought the way we teamed up with Mrs. Ackert, our English and social-studies co-teacher, would make for the most ideal situation. High expectations for all.

In December, Ms. Waldman started using her sick days continuously, showing up occasionally with a hospital-issued respirator that hummed while she gasped for air. In January she asked for a leave of absence. We all prepared for the worst. Mrs. Ackert took over teaching English to our students, wrapping up the unit on *To Kill a Mockingbird*. By the second semester, though, we got exciting news: she was back to full health. Once a week she came to visit the school, glowing, with a new wig, ready to teach. Hugs and love rained on her from students, teachers, and other staff members, even the ones who didn't like her disposition in school. She resumed her duties as curriculum developer, and had every intention of starting school September 1, 2012.

In the meantime, JJ, who kept agitating the local police, finally broke the bull's back and was transferred to a suspension school. His absence from class 814 was palpable. My math-coaching duties often came second to serving as a father figure for the kids.

This class served as the backdrop for my profile in the book *Teacherpreneurs*, by Barnett Berry, Ann Byrd, and Alan Wieder. Berry wanted to profile my school because of the different types of innovative teacher leadership our principal had put together and because of how many of us have some role in how the school functions. I told the staff that Barnett and Wieder would come to profile the school. It turned out that they wanted to focus specifically on me. I knew I had a good rapport with my colleagues but, as with everything, I knew my victories came in the classroom with my students. This was the first class I had felt comfortable introducing to my world outside of school. At this point in my career I still felt odd asking people to visit my classroom—not because I had something to hide from my colleagues, but because I didn't want to mix the world I had developed inside school with the one outside school. The persona I created online and the professional I created inside of school needed to find a meeting point and this class felt like the perfect one. When the authors visited, this class conveyed my passion for teaching much better than anything I could have said.

We threw birthday parties and prepped the kids for prom and graduation. But we did it without Ms. Waldman and JJ.

In June, a few kids in our class prepared a special award for Ms. Waldman at graduation. She mustered enough energy to go and the kids reciprocated with love and tears. The principal wanted to dedicate the renovated library to her name in honor of her tireless dedication to her kids. She gave the equivalent of an "Aw shucks" and thanked everyone quickly. She couldn't *stand* all this attention and soon left the sweltering auditorium.

Over the summer, her cancer overcame her and in August Ms. Waldman passed away. At her funeral, I saw fellow staff members, including my principal, but I didn't want them to see anything other than my professional mask. I only wanted Luz and Mr. Herrera sitting next to me. As rabbis and loved ones spoke about Ms. Waldman, I held my face in my hands, hoping to catch some air while I dried my eyes.

Even at her ceremony, she was teaching me to breathe and let go.

A few months later, I was walking down the hallway when I caught JJ in the corner of my eye. He sat next to our dean with a sly smile. We shook hands and spoke for a little while before I rushed to my next class. I put my hand on his shoulder and told him, "Glad to see you. Welcome home." He nodded and said, "Thank you." We hadn't had a pleasant conversation since September 2011.

I want to tell you it gets better from here, but, just as I couldn't reach him, neither could the teachers who came after me. Soon I saw a picture of him floating around with a blunt in his mouth, left middle finger extended, a gang sign on his right hand. A year later one of his running buddies from eighth grade turned his life around and began working toward culinary school. He told us that JJ had recently suffered a broken leg after sliding off a fire escape. I felt bad—until he explained that JJ had been robbing his neighbor's house and was trying to escape when the accident happened. He was arrested and hospitalized at the same time.

One of the last things Elana Waldman told me about JJ was: "Justin pissed me off today! God! With the talking and the bothering other kids! What is his problem?" She giggled. She rolled her eyes. She took a deep breath. Then said, "You gotta love him." We both shook our heads. If Ms. Waldman had been alive, she would have asked us to go visit JJ with her, to send him letters, to wake up earlier for work to make sure there weren't any others like him.

WHY TEACH?

Teacher Qualifications

Prepare to sacrifice three-fourths of your day and your
    life to the world's noblest profession
While the other fourth you're wondering where the
    time went
In a permanent classroom where your first name no
    longer means much
In the hallway where everyone's business becomes yours
In the staircase where you can be yourself but not really
In the home wondering where the bottom of the pile
    of papers lies
In the street where you become your own personal
    public relations rep
In the professional development meeting where acronyms
    and synonyms get flung with an understanding that
    no one really understands
Political demands and children's actual needs meet in a
    crossroad
Push pressure points to both sides of that fork
Enough pressure to crush rocks,
But instead of building jewels, it creates jade
While outsiders perceive this profession as a game of
    spades
Takes a true master of cards to keep a full deck

When a bit of respect is paramount, tantamount
To succeed in this job
Prepare yourself for the drama, the broken hearts in class,
The bottomless pit of socio-emotional-academic
        deficiencies
Wave goodbye to sleep, to sleep, to sleep
To subjectivity and absolute autonomy
But most importantly, prepare yourself for the inevitability
Of a transformation process in which you learn more
        than your students do
Regardless of whether you suck or not
Develop standards higher than you've ever stretched
        your arms to
Measure your self-worth in less customary terms
In nineties instead of degrees
In hands raised instead of feet
In steps up instead of salary steps
In percentage of students finding positive success rather
        than the range of scores accumulated from a state
        test everyone's pressured to take
The same pressure jade is made from
And the same pressure real diamonds pop from
The type whose teacher qualifications can't be put in a
        rubric
Who students were right about
From the moment they sat down in that classroom
And said, "I really need your help. And I'm ready to learn."

The most ubiquitous question that every teacher faces has to be
Why do you teach? The last person who asked me this genuinely
wanted to know why I would choose a profession in which there
is so much at stake and so little reward. Half the time I can't tell
whether the person's asking out of admiration or pity. While teachers consistently rank among the highest in public-servant approval

ratings, a small contingent of influential naysayers often complains about teachers getting summers off and never shouldering accountability for student learning.

After coming along on this journey with me, I hope you've gotten a sense of what it is like to teach—not just in urban schools, but within the parameters of any space in which we are beholden to a certain set of children, a certain set of adults, and a certain set of conditions. These are the variables that determine the type of teacher you become. And of course, the teacher you become is an extension of the person you are at that moment.

It is also an extension of your own time as a student. Those years absolutely determine how you *think* you will approach teaching. But once you are on the other side of the teacher-student relationship, you realize how demanding it is. You're the one setting up that beautiful classroom. You're the one ultimately determining what thirty students learn on a particular day. If you were the good student growing up, you're now the teacher ensuring that you're properly growing in your academic knowledge. If you were the misbehaving student, you're going to get a good dose of your own medicine.

But as a former "bad student," you might also have an opportunity to relate to the harder-to-reach students. You can help mitigate some of the socio-emotional challenges they can't verbalize yet. You're no silver bullet, but you can help guide them along the right paths.

You might be wondering why I would try to convince you to teach, or even why you would ever want to. The landscape of the profession looks bleak right now. In New York and Los Angeles, teachers can't rely on the law to protect them from the local media publicizing arbitrary numbers as a measure of their supposed success in the classroom—or lack thereof. People trust their local teachers more than they trust most institutions, including the president and local politicians, but they can't escape the barrage of teacher-blaming in the national media. The government has more money for weapons than for schools or to keep kids from coming to class hungry. Teacher salaries remain low.

I'm still hopeful.

It's also true that the average Juan can list his favorite (and not-so-favorite) teachers, people who usually had a greater influence on their lives than even the teachers themselves recognize.

I've come a long way from the Lillian Wald projects on the Lower East Side. Growing up I saw enough roses, hearses, ambulances, arrests, little blue bags, single mothers, and blue, green, purple, and red caps to write my own gangsta rap. (I tried to rap but that never panned out. Stage-name issues, I think.) Some of the kids I grew up with were considered crack babies; some of my cousins came in and out of jail like shoppers at the Macy's in Herald Square. I slept with the sounds of gunshots and arguments outside my window and woke up with the smog of ashes blowing right in. I'm proud to have risen above all that—and I have educators to thank for keeping me from becoming a statistic. There were times when the only sanity I could find was in the rituals and routines we had in school. Whether it was reciting the morning Pledge of Allegiance in elementary school or the Our Father every day at Nativity, I knew what to expect. I knew that when I walked into an academic building, there'd be bells ringing, floors sneaker-squeaking, and pencils scratching paper. These sounds brought me comfort and safety the way nine-millimeters don't.

But it didn't happen on its own. Educators created that environment.

When I ask most of my friends exactly what they learned from their favorite (or least favorite) teacher, they have a hard time remembering the academic lessons. But they can enumerate and expound on the interpersonal experiences they had with that teacher. They wax poetic about the teachers they loved, cringe and clench their teeth at the teachers they reviled. When we teach, we don't *just* teach them the subjects; we implicitly teach them customs, rituals, and character traits that they either emulate or admire in their own right.

Even the teachers I hated had some influence on why and how I teach. I didn't have the language to say this, but somehow I knew I could do a much better job—and make a career out of doing it better.

Every student, afforded the right amount of patience and understanding, has the ability to excel. Every teacher, with the right qualities, can contribute to a student's growth as a citizen of the planet. Teaching and learning are amorphous, but when they're happening the symbiosis is undeniable.

This is why I teach: It is not just a job for me, it's also an understanding that I'll pay forward all the awesome gifts I've been given. As much as people might try to make education a more scientific profession, where data is king and jargon is queen, teachers exist to cultivate kids the way farmers cultivate crops. Technologies change, chemicals change, and the earth changes, but the relationship between a farmer and her harvest comes out in the texture and zing of the crop.

My kids don't want teachers telling them to change who they are, either. We New Yorkers get really testy when people try to change us. Kids from my hood are guarded against their teachers unless they have a cultural connection or are able to develop a relationship that transcends their differences. If a kid shows a creative side, teachers ought to push them to develop it and relate it to what they're doing in class. I was a sucker for my Irish-American English teacher, who quipped to me when I was a sophomore, "So you're saying that rap music isn't poetry on some level?" I loved when my high-school drama teacher laid out Shakespearean curses on her wall right around the time I learned how to rap along with Biggie's *Life After Death*. After losing my school's seventh-grade spelling bee—I was a finalist and battled for a good thirty minutes—Ms. Miranda, my English teacher, gave me a book on common words to enhance my vocabulary over winter vacation. Even in the blazing sun of Santo Domingo, I'd sit on the porch and tear through thirty pages a day. These teachers didn't try to change me; they just presented opportunities for exploration and motivation. They said, "You seem like you'd be really good at this. Try it and tell me what you think."

I did my part too, of course. I worked hard for the majority of my academic career. I ran into trouble, though; the same Catholic school teachers who held me in high esteem gave me JUG so much, I almost thought those were my initials.* But when I needed a pat on the back, I got it. I remember my teachers' ability to make me feel like everything I had to say was important; my thoughts mattered in and out of the classroom to them. It didn't matter if my voice broke through puberty, if I stuttered through a speech, or if I just needed to speak as a distraction from my home situation. For someone who didn't understand yet the power of voice, it meant a lot.

Teaching grasps the soul like a finger probing, not clenching, the heart. It begs you to advocate on behalf of the children, even when you least expect to. Teachers learn to be selfless, to deliver sincerely no matter what's happening in their personal lives. Despite my difficulties with my homeroom, my administration, or other teachers, when I walk into my classroom I'm given another reason to love what I do. I rarely ever have two bad days in a row (or else!). I love walking into school knowing that it's not going to be the same exact job it was a day, a month, or a year ago. A student always finds a way to inspire me or crack me the hell up. The only real feedback I need is from the students in front of me.

Teaching has given me no choice but to activate my best inner qualities and to accept and embrace that I will never stop being a student myself. I love that every day there's a new set of problems for me to solve. Even as I'm teaching my kids math, I'm learning along with them.

In the future the academic and pedagogical skills a teacher needs may change, but the foundation of love, respect, passion, and curiosity remains. Yes, most of us agree that we need to challenge

---

* "JUG," for those of you unfamiliar, is a Catholic-school term for detention. Rumor has it that JUG is also an acronym for "justice under God."

the current curricula and push beyond rote memorization. Yes, when most of us say that schools aren't working, we're mostly referring to schools in high-poverty areas. Yes, our approaches to this vision differ in scope and ideology. No, none of this should discourage you from becoming a teacher.

I hope that becoming a key player in the lives of hundreds of students a year will fuel your fire—knowing that it's not enough to simply do, but that you must leave a legacy of doing. As a teacher you will play such an important part in your students' lives that even when they forget the specifics of what you taught them, they'll remember the feelings and life lessons you left them with, the impression that someone other than their parents (if applicable) cared enough to spur them toward their own successes.

You can make the difference. You can prompt students to ask critical questions. You can inspire them to aspire. You can help others understand the true importance of education. You can be as realistic about our country's expectations and as idealistic about our children's futures as you need to be.

If you *can't* teach, you do. Something else, preferably. But if you can't do, then don't. As a teacher, I'm in charge of believing you can—so do. If you plan to do, then do this.

Go hard or go home.

CONCLUSION:
A NOTE FROM THIS NATIVE SON

On the morning of July 13, 2013, I woke up and gasped a brisk breath in our dimly lit, air-conditioned hotel room in Cocoa Beach, Florida. My mind and heart wanted to know. I couldn't find the remote, but I found my phone. I hit the Twitter app because if the decision came as I thought it would, I could only stand 140 characters.

"Oh nooooo . . ." I whispered.

That was enough. I hopped back into bed and my mind went black. My son woke up and squeaked from his makeshift crib. Luz didn't see the commotion, but understood shortly thereafter. The idea that a Black boy could get shot just because he "looked like a criminal" pissed me off, but allowing a man to get away with murdering a Black boy made our criminal justice system complicit in the murder. It revealed to me something I always found true about myself: consciousness about our status in this country means harboring a permanent, simmering sense of anger and resentment about our second-class citizenship, triggered by people turned events: Emmett Till, Renisha McBride, Jordan Davis, Latasha Harlins, Oscar Grant. If the American justice system couldn't find justice for Trayvon, those of us who wanted it would.

I held my son tightly while I listened to reactions to the verdict. I was afraid to so much as open the curtains; I didn't feel like participating in any of the makeshift memorial services and marches occurring an hour's drive from where we were staying. I had a full week of professional development and STEM-related activities planned, and José the humanitarian would have to take a backseat to Mr. Vilson the professional—for now. But, truth be told, Sybrina Fulton and Tracy Martin's pain mattered more than any individual or collective politics at that moment.

People who claimed that Martin wasn't innocent painted a picture of a kid who somehow deserved to die for mistakes they themselves might have made in their youth. Should they too have been shot for their teenage transgressions? Imagine your heroes, those who have inspired us and changed the world. What if we had shot them in their teens without thinking of what they might have gone on to do? What if Nelson Mandela's life had ended at the hands of a George Zimmerman?

In his autobiographical *Notes of a Native Son*, James Baldwin wrote that the Negro

> is a social and not a personal or a human problem; to think of him is to think of statistics, slums, rapes, injustices, remote violence; it is to be confronted with an endless cataloguing of losses, gains, skirmishes; it is to feel virtuous, outraged, helpless, as though his continuing status among us were somehow analogous to disease—cancer, perhaps, or tuberculosis—which must be checked, even though it cannot be cured. In this arena the black man acquires quite another aspect from that which he has in life. We do not know what to do with him in life; if he breaks our sociological and sentimental image of him we are panic-stricken and we feel ourselves betrayed. When he violates this image, therefore, he stands in the greatest danger (sensing which, we uneasily suspect that he is very often playing a part for our benefit); and, what is not always so apparent but is equally true, we are then in some danger ourselves—hence our retreat or our blind and immediate retaliation.[*]

I'm fighting for the right for us to see each other as multidimensional, to resist the stereotype, the statistic, what Zimmerman, his defense attorneys, and our national media made Trayvon.

[*] James Baldwin, *Notes of a Native Son* (Boston: Beacon Press, 2012), 26.

I think of Mandela now because his death coincided with another loss. When news of his passing flashed across my TV screen as I watched ESPN, I had taken a personal day from work to privately mourn the loss of another gigantic figure in my life: my father. Juliot Vilson, a man survived by seven children spread across New York City and Miami, died of heart failure on December 3, 2013. As I write this, I can feel the effects of his passing: conflicting emotions, among them the feeling that I should not mourn him to begin with. I saw him once a year, if that. Our reunions felt like bookmarks in a story not fully written, forever-incomplete pages in my understanding of this man.

As a child I longed for him, wishing he would visit more regularly. I didn't know that he had "put hands" on my mother or that at the time I was born he already had an older son in Haiti (James) and a six-month-old daughter in Miami (Patricia). Even if I had, even though he did nothing to stop my stepfather from trying to beat me in his drunken rage, should I have stopped talking to him? Should I have let him rot instead of visiting him in the hospital after his first heart attack? Should I have shut him out for not saying a word when my son Alejandro was born?

Should I not look at the skin I'm in because looking at myself is the only time I see him?

I remember the times we *did* spend together, at house parties and bars with live bands when I was eight or fifteen. He always came off as the life of the party, with the irrepressible energy he gave off to women and the alpha-male handshake he gave to men. As he danced, drank, and smoked cigarettes, I closed my eyes and wished to spend time with him in a different way, to make up for the time we missed. But that wasn't him. He had a furious side that his closest family saw, a playful side that his lovers saw, and a rare paternal side that only a couple of his children saw consistently. All of these encompassed him, so that's how I choose to remember him.

These collective experiences—lived and witnessed—nudged me to make my existence in the classroom one of caretaker, observer, protector. At its most revolutionary, the women and men of color in any field see themselves collectively as the spiritual mothers and fathers of those who seek to come afterward. As a teacher of color, sharing a lived experience with your students makes it imperative to do your best for your students. That personal dimension is often missing when you don't.

Without knowing it, not having a consistent father figure forced me to fill the void by taking on that responsibility in the classroom, guiding youth the way I would my own daughter or son. When I thought about all the young men and women who passed through my classroom the morning of the trial and acquittal, I saw students equally susceptible to success and to murder, depending on who was handing out diplomas and who was behind the gun. My job is to lead them on the path to success knowing full well that, systemically, the odds are truly against them.

I can't compartmentalize my experiences and education inside and outside the classroom. To do so might make life easier; it might make me more palatable to people in power. I don't have a choice in how people perceive me before I speak or act, but I do have a choice in how I react and how I identify and share my own experiences.

When the sun came up, Luz laid next to me. We held Alejandro close for most of the morning while we listened to analyst after blustering analyst subtly rejoice that they had been right all along. I kept hoping Alé's olive skin tone could withstand society's implicit perceptions of him. Thus, on a bright summer day in Cocoa Beach, Florida, just as on a cloudy, rainy December day in New York City later that year, I was inclined to wear all black. I always do.

AFTERWORD

I have been teaching in various capacities and at various levels—preschool, elementary, middle, high school, undergraduate, and graduate school—for more than thirty years. I was drawn to teach because I saw it as a concrete way to have an impact on the things I cared about, namely the suffering in Black and Latino communities. I thought that through teaching I could have a concrete impact on people and conditions; that prospect has kept me in this profession.

Despite my commitment to teaching, I am not naïve. As a sociologist, I know the research, and for more than fifty years the data has revealed the same thing: rather than serving as a pathway to opportunity, more often than not education reproduces existing patterns of inequality.

Certainly, there are exceptions. I count myself as one. I grew up poor in Brownsville, Brooklyn (Tilden Houses), and though unlike many of my peers I had two parents (and most importantly a father with a good working-class job—a New York City police officer), neither of my parents graduated from high school. The fact that I went to Brown for my bachelor's and master's degrees, received my doctorate from Berkeley, and went on to be a professor at Berkeley, Harvard, and now New York University is further proof that education can serve as a vehicle to a more privileged life.

Except I know the data. For every social climber like me, there are literally thousands of others who remain in the class of their parents, who never escape the projects, the ghetto, the *barrio*, the trailer park, or any of the other poor and working-class communities that limit, entrap, and marginalize.

Knowing the data and related research as I do, one might ask why I still believe in education. After reading *This Is Not a Test*, I am reminded of why I stay in the field. Through his experience as a teacher and a young man of color growing up in the segregated communities of New York City, José Vilson reminds us why education matters. He also shows us that teachers can have a critical voice in the national conversation about the future of public education— and that when they are not afraid, they can use that voice to challenge the way systematic inequality in education reproduces itself.

Like me, Vilson also understands the limitations of public education. As a professional teacher, he lives it. He is forced to administer the tests that are used to rank and judge his students rather than help them. He is forced to work in schools that stifle creativity through their fixation on conformity and control; he is an eyewitness to the suffering his students endure as they pass through schools that, more often than not, keep them in their place.

However, Vilson is much more than a cog in the system. As a blogger, an educator, and an activist, Vilson has found a way to express the outrage and frustration that teachers like him endure. He stands as an ally with his students and the communities he serves as he uses his "teacher voice" to speak out about the injustices perpetuated in the name of reform. He is determined not to be complicit in the reproduction of inequality. He is, rather, a subversive who understands that knowledge is power and that, even under the adverse conditions under which he works, there are possibilities for action and resistance.

For this reason, *This Is Not a Test* is more than a memoir; it is a reminder that there are teachers who understand that when the classroom door closes they truly have the power—the power to demonstrate compassion, to connect, to inspire, to challenge, and to critique. He also understands that his power can extend beyond the classroom, as he uses social media to insert himself and the many teachers who identify with him into the national debate over school reform.

For those who have lost hope about the possibility of using education to create a more just and democratic society, this book will be a reminder of what can be achieved when educators act with the courage of their convictions to speak out and write about what is occurring in our schools today. Vilson is a gadfly, an education activist, and a "griot," or spokesman, for all those who are not just tired of the direction our policy makers have taken in the name of reform but are willing to do something to challenge it.

This book and José Vilson's ongoing work remind us that, just as education can be used to dominate, control, and oppress, it can also be used to provoke and liberate. Let us hope that other educators are able to see the power and potential of their voices and join in the struggle to save our schools and our fragile democracy.

Pedro Noguera
Peter L. Agnew Professor of Education, New York University

ACKNOWLEDGMENTS

I have too many people to thank, and if your name is explicitly or implicitly missing, blame my mind and not my heart. Please don't kill my vibe.

First and foremost, I am thankful for the love and patience that Luz, my fiancée, and Alejandro, my son, have had for and with me through this process. I've worked on this manuscript for the better part of four years, but the last couple of months have been particularly sleepless. To them, I dedicate this book. My present. My future. My everything. I love you.

I thank my mother, Milagros, and my brother Ralf for their encouragement and love. Mom, thank you for birthing and raising me. Ralf, keep hustling. Eventually, the light will shine brightly on you. Special shout out to Kevin and the rest of the family as well. Stay up.

To the Rojas family, thank you as well: Blanca Salcedo, Rodrigo Rojas, Gabriel Rojas, Kristin Kahle, and the big boy Brandon. Blanca, that book you gave me a few years ago? Well, guess who published it? *Presagio!*

I'm also thankful for Vanessa, Nathalie, James, Mous, and the entire Vilson clan for the support. It's been good getting reunited in the last decade or so.

I'd also like to thank the extended families: Zuleika Martinez (*coma'i!*) and Melissa and Paul Melkonian (and the babies: Miles and Liam and . . .). Special hello to AnnMary, Ray, Jo Jo, GiGi, and the whole Yuen-Parker collective.

225

I thank my principal, Dr. Sal Fernandez, and the entire IS 52 family past and present. Without you, I wouldn't have become the educator I am today, so thanks. I'm eternally grateful to call so many of you colleagues, mentors, and friends. It's always nerve-wracking when one of your teachers is writing a book about school, but I hope this was true to the message of elevating us.

I thank the good folks at Haymarket Books. A special shout-out to super-publisher Julie Fain, who was the last publisher I would have pitched to before I self-published this. You took a huge risk in taking this teacher into your camp at a time when people are afraid (AFRAID!) to take on a current educator of color to write books about their stories. Jim Plank, Anthony Arnove, Eric Kerl, Rory Fanning, Jason Farbman, Rachel Cohen, and Brian Baughan, thank you for putting your hearts and minds into this project. To special-super editor Liliana Segura: thank you thank you thank you. Admittedly, your edits hurt like hell, but this book and I are better for it. The last two months of the editing process were wild for both of us personally and professionally, but I wouldn't have it any other way. To Sarah Grey: not only did you help refine my manuscript, you also managed to get us into the *Chicago Manual of Style*. History-making!

To University Settlement Head Start, the Nathan Strauss School (PS 140), Nativity Mission School, Xavier High School, Syracuse University, and City College of New York and all the people associated with these institutions: each of you had a hand in my current success, and I'm thankful to everyone who brought me along this path.

To the United Federation of Teachers, American Federation of Teachers, New York State United Teachers, and National Education Association: thanks for assuring that this teacher gets to whisper, yell, and everything in between for the improvement of public education.

Also, to Karen Lewis and Pedro Noguera: thank you for blessing us all with your words of encouragement in this book and for your own work. You both have no idea how much you continue to inspire those working to do right by our most marginalized voices.

I thank, in no particular order, the following very special people for their inspiration, words of encouragement, and for reading my book and telling me whether or not I should publish it: Indira Gil, Chris Lehmann, Sabrina Stevens, Liz Dwyer, Melinda Anderson, Renee Moore, Eva Haldane, Jessica Filion, Raquel Cepeda, Arthur Goldstein, Gregory Michie, Alexa Muñoz, John Holland (. . . ahem, *Dr.* John Holland, so proud), Aurelia Flores, Shannon C'de Baca, Amauri Tavarez, Lucia Chan, Tafari Stevenson-Howard, Xian Barrett, Jason Buell, Audrey Watters, Kelvin Oliver, Rameer Green, Leslie Grinner, Michael Klonsky, Jonathan Halabi, Nancy Flanagan, Michael Doyle, John Spencer, Bill Ivey, Diana Laufenberg, Basil Kolani, Christopher Emdin, Holly Epstein Ojalvo, Jonathan Serrano, Steven Lazar, Ariel Sacks, Cindi Rigsbee, Leo Casey, Bill Fitzgerald, Rafranz Davis, Stephanie Rivera, Mike Thayer, Cecelia Durazo, Ynanna Djehuty, Papo Swiggity, John "Chance" Acevedo, and the late John Rodriguez.

To my Center for Teaching Quality family, Barnett Berry, Ann Byrd, Arthur Wise, and everyone at Carrboro, North Carolina, thank you for embracing me and my M&M-devouring ways. I'm so appreciative of you all, and here's hoping we have more years of calamari and purple-green paraphernalia. To Betty Ray and my *Edutopia* folk, thanks for letting me parody Robert Marzano and the Wu-Tang Clan on your platform. They will never be ready for us, but you took me in anyway. Badass.

To Dennis Van Roekel, Randi Weingarten, and Diane Ravitch: thank you for your work in the service of improving public schools. Let's keep working on this for all kids.

Tara Betts, you've been an inspiration to me since I first found your poems. Thank you for that first real read-through of my manuscript and for your continued support of my work. I'm eternally grateful. Harmony McGuire, there would be no *The Jose Vilson* without you. You didn't let me quit. Actually, you laughed me off when I tried to. Shame on you, and thanks. Amber Cabral, I've always wanted to achieve your level of writing, so sincere and soulful. I hope I did right by you with this one.

To John Norton: you've worked in the background in the role of constant curator. With me, you served as a guru and gentle ass-kicker. Actually, I think your words were:

> Don't imitate. Don't write things that are purely polemical because some members of your political family offer atta-way points for doing so. If you're not bringing some fresh perspective—some unique—to it, it just ends up on the big pile of "there's another one." . . . Your writing seems most powerful and insightful—"changeful"—when you step back/up and become the observer, narrating the story of The Jose Vilson with a critical eye. In guru-speak, your "higher self" is doing the writing . . . and I don't think it's any secret, if you read accounts of other good writers doing their work, that this is when the good stuff flows. Some would call it "channeling your soul" and others "opening a vein." Same result, I think.

I've been thanking you ever since.

To my students: thank you for having me as your teacher. Not that you had a choice, but I felt privileged to teach each and every one of you. You aren't always named, but you'll never be nameless. Live on.

INDEX

229

ABOUT THE AUTHOR

José Luis Vilson is a math educator, blogger, speaker, and activist in New York City. He has written about education, math, and race for a number of organizations and publications, including the *New York Times*, *Education Week*, the *Huffington Post*, *Edutopia*, *GOOD*, and *El Diario/La Prensa*. His blog, *The Jose Vilson*, is at www.thejosevilson.com. He can be found on Twitter and Facebook as @TheJLV. He lives with his fiancée and son in El Barrio/Harlem, NY.